INFINITE SISTERS

A Story of Friendship (and Loss)

Megan May

with Stephen May

NO DIRECTION PRESS // XD 004

Copyediting by Carrie Bond.
Cover design by Beth Sullivan.
Cover illustration by Adrenalinapura Professional Photography & Design.

ISBN: 978-0-6997-9086-4

Happy Reading Drew ♡ xo Megan May

"When someone you love becomes a memory,
that memory becomes a treasure."
— Unknown

For Kennedy, Daunte, Iris, Craig, and Ryan

INTRODUCTION

Mary Elizabeth Johnson Blocher and I were born with the same middle name not quite a year apart. I arrived first, on July 21, 1974. Mary followed on June 17, 1975. We grew up a few towns away from each other in the hills southeast of Pittsburgh.

Mary's dad, Donald, a retired steelworker, served as an associate pastor at the Christian Center Church in Belle Vernon, Pennsylvania. Mary's mother, Marlene, worked as a food service supervisor at Jefferson Hospital and volunteered as a welcome room attendant at church. My parents, Joe and Janet, were both teachers: my dad at Knoxville Middle School, not far from Mount Oliver, which both was and wasn't in Pittsburgh[1], and my mom at Mount

---

[1] There are actually two Mount Olivers: a larger borough, surrounded on all sides by Pittsburgh, and a smaller,

Lebanon High School, where she worked with visually impaired students. Mary and I each had three siblings. Mary was the baby, coming after Craig, Karen, and Iris; I was the middle sister, born between sister Jenny and brother Stephen, with Katie Beth occupying Mary's "baby" slot.

Our backgrounds were not without their differences—not least among them that Mary was Black and I was White—but there were also many similarities. We both came from large families, had close relationships with our older sisters, and had been brought up around the arts—theater in particular. From an early age, we both gravitated to the stage. In high school, we were both theater kids with an affinity for musicals. My senior year, I saw Mary perform as Dorothy in *The Wizard of Oz* at her high school, Elizabeth Forward. I was floored by Mary's powerful voice; I told anyone who would listen that this person was a *star*.

Mary and I officially met a few months later, in the fall of 1993, during orientation at Point Park College in Downtown Pittsburgh. We were both musical theater majors. No one goes into college with a fine arts major without a chorus of

---

adjacent neighborhood that is part of the City of Pittsburgh. My dad grew up in the former.

I stare at the ceiling. I tune out the sounds of the ICU. Tomorrow afternoon we will walk to the surgery room. You selflessly donated all of your organs. They will take you off all the machines and I will lose my person.

My mind travels back to tell our story; there is so much to tell about you, about decades of friendship! I'm gonna tell our story, Mare Mare, even if nobody reads it. My mind travels back . . .

ACT 1: SWINBURNE SISTERS

PROLOGUE

Mare Mare. We are together again hanging out, listening to Aretha Franklin. You have a beautiful new manicure, blue and sparkly like a winter angel, compliments of our talented friend, Janice. Your hair is in your eye; you are in your "platinum blonde" stage still. As a true bestie, I brush the hair away. I am talking to you, dishing out the latest gossip, telling you what happened at work, asking for your expert Mare advice on my latest dilemma. As always, I feel safe, like I'm not being judged. We are more than friends, more than family. We are simply soulmates, like we knew each other in a past life. Outsiders, jealous of our connection, have even suggested that it is romantic, which is ridiculous. We are best friends.

I take a sip of my drink, scan the room for a clock. There is a very big difference between this and our million other hangs. We are not in my living room sipping Moscato, eating white cheddar Skinny Pop Popcorn, laughing our asses off, watching *Keeping Up with the Kardashians*. I am holding your hand in the intensive care unit, where you have been the whole week, non-responsive.

You had COVID-19, but, unlike so many others, you didn't get better. It seems like just yesterday that you turned a corner: you were up on your feet a little, off oxygen, eating a meal. The night brought three heart attacks and a massive stroke attacking one side of your body. You had always been feisty, a fighter, but the virus had worn down your tiny body.

Now you can only squeeze my hand and stare at me with a look of calm and recognition. I have already lost you. Your essence is gone. God is calling you home.

Why? You are forty-six. Your children need you. You still need to record an album with that one-of-a-kind voice of yours. We have so many adventures ahead. You are supposed to be in the retirement home with me someday, roommates again, octogenarians in high heels causing trouble. I have already lost my baby sister, aged thirty-four, to a tragedy. This can't be happening. I squeeze your hand and you grip mine back. Is this just a reflex? Are you in there?

doubters following behind, questioning such a so-called foolish decision. But Mary and I had only ever dreamed of being performers. There would be time later in life for finding a more "serious" vocation, if necessary. We were going to try to do it our way, first.

I soon found myself gravitating toward character roles, and Mary established herself as the first-year student with the voice. What made Mary's singing so special was her combination of power and control. Mary had pipes throughout her range, but she also had the artistic touch of supremely talented singers like Whitney Houston. And Mary's stage presence had the same glow as her voice. I loved every chance I got to share the stage with her.

My first-year roommate was a fellow actor and friend from high school. Things started off great, but before long there was friction. Though we would continue to be friends, sharing a room was not working out. Mary just so happened to have a single room on my same floor, and it became a place of refuge for me. Mary's personality matched her voice: She was strong, beautiful, and room-filling in the best way possible. Not only that, she was warm, funny, and easy to talk to. What began as daily sanity checks for me soon became a friendship, with Mary's room as our headquarters.

The summer after our second year, Mary and I both knew we wanted to move "onward and upward" out of the dorms. This was back when you still had to find "for rent" listings in the classified section of the local newspaper—in our case the *Pittsburgh Post-Gazette*. Finally, through one of my dad's teacher connections, we found a first-floor place in a brick house at the corner of Swinburne and Dawson Street in Pittsburgh's South Oakland neighborhood. Though it wasn't especially close to school, the place had the advantage of being an easy walk up the Boulevard of the Allies to the Pittsburgh Playhouse, where Point Park's theater program held its performances. Our place soon became a go-to spot for our fellow actors, and we hosted several memorable parties.

What followed was our own version of the 1988 drama *Beaches*. Mary and I forged parallel paths into the world. We took jobs near each other and acted together as often as possible. We were adopted members of each other's extended families, and our husbands, Steve and Ryan, were also best friends. We bought houses a couple of towns over from each other. We had our babies together—first two girls, then two boys. We vacationed together. Mary picked me up off the floor when my sister Katie died, and I was there for her when she lost her parents and her beloved sister, Karen.

Over time, Mary and I continued to grow closer. We spoke every day and hung out weekly. During the COVID-19 lockdown, we even FaceTimed to drink wine and laugh until we cried tears of joy, amusement, and healing.

Mary's passing felt like losing a costar: I was Cindy Williams without Penny Marshall, Lucille Ball without Vivian Vance. In the blurry months after Mary's death, I spoke with a grief counselor who suggested that I use my creativity and my memories of joyful times with Mary to keep her close to me, to keep the flame of our friendship alive in my heart. For more than a year, I wrote one story a week.

My initial intent was to write to heal my own heart. As the project grew in scope, though, it took on another purpose: to give Mary, and our friendship, new life. Through retelling the story of my friendship with Mary, I have recorded it for posterity. I have also attempted to effect a transfiguration from friend and friendship into essence. I want to give Mary's children, and the other people who knew and loved her, an idea of the singular person Mary to me was through our years of knowing each other. I wrote these stories with Mary's children, Kennedy and Daunte; her husband, Ryan; and her surviving sister, Iris, and brother, Craig, in my heart.

state, I persisted with reason: "Maybe you dropped it on your walk back; we can retrace your steps together and see if we can find it."

Mary now crossed over, fleetingly, from anger into despondency: "Oh JESUS, TAKE ME! MY FUCKING BUS PASS! I JUST BOUGHT IT! I DON'T HAVE FIFTY DOLLARS. MORE TO SPEND! I'M GONNA MISS CLASS EVERY DAY!"

She returned to rage—"SON OF A BITCH!"—and began slamming her books and notebooks around the floor.

It was at this point that I decided to disengage: Clearly, Mary needed a moment.

I grabbed the phone book and our cordless phone and tiptoed out the kitchen door to my favorite, little bench under the single tree in our yard. I looked up the Port Authority and left a message putting out the alert for the missing pass. Then, I thought about the businesses on our regular walk home from the bus stop. There was a medical diagnostics place; I didn't really know what they actually did, but hey, it was worth a shot. The secretary picked up and instantly knew what I was talking about: A Good Samaritan in the form of a patient had found the pass on the sidewalk and brought it in, thinking that maybe it belonged to an employee. I had struck gold!

Triumphantly, I clicked the cordless phone off and pressed the antenna into "resting" position. I returned to the kitchen to find Mary still muttering to herself, methodically flipping through the pages of her textbooks. "THEY HAVE THE BUS PASS!" I mouthed.

And, instantly, Mary was Mary. "What?! Who has my bus pass, Meg?"

"The medical diagnostics place!"

"What medical diagnostics place?!"

I explained my phone-call approach to Mary. She hugged me and called me the kinds of things—*smart, organized, calm*—that I too rarely called myself. I felt resplendently alive, almost aglow.

Then I noticed the smell of burning cheese: the pizza squares!

At the medical diagnostics place, as gray and nondescript as its name would suggest, we were received as minor celebrities: the bus pass people. Mary, who felt everything *more*, was as gracious with the receptionist as she had been apoplectic in the apartment just a few minutes before. If cell phones had existed, they would have posed for a selfie.

That night we treated ourselves to margaritas and taco salads at our favorite restaurant, Mad Mex, an easy walk from our place. No bus passes required.

2. "NUTTY PROFESSOR"

With "Contact-gate" behind us, the rest of Mary's time in *Tintypes* should have been no problem. Not exactly. The next week, Mary came down with really bad bronchitis. In the times before COVID, the show was going to go on, regardless of the health of the performer. Because no one wanted to hear "Sometimes, I Feel Like a Motherless Child" croaked out by a performer in obvious discomfort, actors desperately sought out medical interventions. Mary was being treated with steroid shots and antibiotics to bring back her epic, show-stopping voice. The meds did the trick for the voice but didn't come without a downside.

At the time I was in the middle of one of my two tenures at Accentricity, a jewelry kiosk in Station Square. Looking back, I don't know how I survived the various, random jobs I had. At Accentricity, I somehow learned to customize gold chains and change watch batteries. Just getting there was like the opening montage in *Flashdance*: I had to walk three blocks, take two buses, then cross the Smithfield Street Bridge. One reason I stayed at the job, other than the obvious need for cash, was my beautiful, sweet boss, Carol Wilson, who felt like family.

On this particular night, I came home around one to a panic-stricken Mary calling from the living room: "MEG, MY LIPS. Please go get my Claritin, please! My lips are swollen!"

I didn't have time to assess the situation; I just ran to the cabinet to get the medicine and stopped in the kitchen to grab a drink for Mary.

On entering the living room, I honestly was not prepared to see what I saw. Under normal circumstances, Mary's lips were full and beautiful, the kind people get collagen injections to have; her face was flawless. It was instantly clear, though, that something had gone badly wrong. Mary's already naturally full lips had swollen to, easily, three times their normal size. Skin was not meant to stretch that much; it looked painful and, honestly, not good.

As I handed Mary her Claritin and a drink to chug, I tried to manifest calm. I was hoping for a very rapid improvement; Mary, though, was not helping matters.

"Meg, be honest: I look like The Nutty Professor, don't I?"

To make the situation worse, Mary's speech was impaired by the swelling. The effect was reminiscent of the time my childhood next-door neighbor, Eleni, had her jaws wired shut and could only consume liquefied food through a straw.

I took a breath. I had to clench my teeth to suppress a laugh. "I mean, there is a slight Nutty Professor resemblance, but you're much, much cuter. And, hey, at least it's just a swollen lip, not a swollen everything." Then I added, to soften the blow, "You love Eddie Murphy, Mare!"

I thought Mary might have one of her Jesus moments; instead, the room filled with her trademark cackle, unhindered by the swollen mess of her lips. I couldn't help but laugh at Mary's laugh and how ludicrous the situation was. Before long, we were both laughing so hard that we had tears in our eyes.

We devoted the rest of the night to a *Clueless* and *Friday* double feature on our couch. For a while in our first year on Swinburne Street, we watched one or both every night we didn't have

"WHERE THE FUCK IS IT?" Mary muttered to herself as she sifted through her scattered possessions.

As Mary's best friend, I could usually spot when Mary, true to her Gemini nature, was headed in the "Ms. Hyde" direction and try to intervene before things really began to go off the rails. In this case, the best I could do was attempt to triage: "Mare, Mare, what are you looking for? I can help you find it!"

I must have sounded to Mary like the person on the other end of the phone in a Peanuts cartoon, because she kept right on screaming, "WHERE IS IT? WHERE IS MY FUCKING BUS PASS? I KNOW SOMEONE PICKED IT UP AND STOLE IT!"

Neither Mary nor I owned a car. Given the distance between Oakland, where our apartment and the Pittsburgh Playhouse were, and Point Park, where our classes were, a monthly bus pass was a necessity: far more cost-effective and convenient than paying with cash and change, which people still used back then.

Having grown up around a number of people with tempers, myself included, I should have realized that Mary was well past the point of no return. Still, out of genuine concern for Mary's to the tub. "Oh THERE you are," I heard Mary say.

"Mary," I said. "Who are you talking to?"

"The damn contact, Meg!" Mary said. "I'm talking to the damn contact that has been missing for a damn year!" She held it up on the tip of her finger like a Bubble Wand bubble. "I once was lost, but now I'm found," Mary boomed. "Was blind, but now I see!"

* * *

The contact was not the only thing Mary lost on Swinburne Street.

One evening, I was waiting for Mary to return home for our family dinner, the pizza squares in the oven. I had become something of an expert—always the perfect amount of "crispy" around the edges.

Mary came bounding through the front door, which opened into the middle of the living room, and stomped into the kitchen in a flustered panic. She tossed her backpack onto the floor and started dumping it out: books, notebooks, folders, retractable pencils, paper clips, loose pieces of paper of unknown origins all fell onto the linoleum grid below.

state, I persisted with reason: "Maybe you dropped it on your walk back; we can retrace your steps together and see if we can find it."

Mary now crossed over, fleetingly, from anger into despondency: "Oh JESUS, TAKE ME! MY FUCKING BUS PASS! I JUST BOUGHT IT! I DON'T HAVE FIFTY DOLLARS. MORE TO SPEND! I'M GONNA MISS CLASS EVERY DAY!"

She returned to rage—"SON OF A BITCH!"—and began slamming her books and notebooks around the floor.

It was at this point that I decided to disengage: Clearly, Mary needed a moment.

I grabbed the phone book and our cordless phone and tiptoed out the kitchen door to my favorite, little bench under the single tree in our yard. I looked up the Port Authority and left a message putting out the alert for the missing pass. Then, I thought about the businesses on our regular walk home from the bus stop. There was a medical diagnostics place; I didn't really know what they actually did, but hey, it was worth a shot. The secretary picked up and instantly knew what I was talking about: A Good Samaritan in the form of a patient had found the pass on the sidewalk and brought it in, thinking that maybe it belonged to an employee. I had struck gold!

Triumphantly, I clicked the cordless phone off and pressed the antenna into "resting" position. I returned to the kitchen to find Mary still muttering to herself, methodically flipping through the pages of her textbooks. "THEY HAVE THE BUS PASS!" I mouthed.

And, instantly, Mary was Mary. "What?! Who has my bus pass, Meg?"

"The medical diagnostics place!"

"What medical diagnostics place?!"

I explained my phone-call approach to Mary. She hugged me and called me the kinds of things—*smart, organized, calm*—that I too rarely called myself. I felt resplendently alive, almost aglow.

Then I noticed the smell of burning cheese: the pizza squares!

At the medical diagnostics place, as gray and nondescript as its name would suggest, we were received as minor celebrities: the bus pass people. Mary, who felt everything *more*, was as gracious with the receptionist as she had been apoplectic in the apartment just a few minutes before. If cell phones had existed, they would have posed for a selfie.

That night we treated ourselves to margaritas and taco salads at our favorite restaurant, Mad Mex, an easy walk from our place. No bus passes required.

2. "NUTTY PROFESSOR"

With "Contact-gate" behind us, the rest of Mary's time in *Tintypes* should have been no problem. Not exactly. The next week, Mary came down with really bad bronchitis. In the times before COVID, the show was going to go on, regardless of the health of the performer. Because no one wanted to hear "Sometimes, I Feel Like a Motherless Child" croaked out by a performer in obvious discomfort, actors desperately sought out medical interventions. Mary was being treated with steroid shots and antibiotics to bring back her epic, show-stopping voice. The meds did the trick for the voice but didn't come without a downside.

At the time I was in the middle of one of my two tenures at Accentricity, a jewelry kiosk in Station Square. Looking back, I don't know how I survived the various, random jobs I had. At Accentricity, I somehow learned to customize gold chains and change watch batteries. Just getting there was like the opening montage in *Flashdance*: I had to walk three blocks, take two buses, then cross the Smithfield Street Bridge. One reason I stayed at the job, other than the obvious need for cash, was my beautiful, sweet boss, Carol Wilson, who felt like family.

On this particular night, I came home around one to a panic-stricken Mary calling from the living room: "MEG, MY LIPS. Please go get my Claritin, please! My lips are swollen!"

I didn't have time to assess the situation; I just ran to the cabinet to get the medicine and stopped in the kitchen to grab a drink for Mary.

On entering the living room, I honestly was not prepared to see what I saw. Under normal circumstances, Mary's lips were full and beautiful, the kind people get collagen injections to have; her face was flawless. It was instantly clear, though, that something had gone badly wrong. Mary's already naturally full lips had swollen to, easily, three times their normal size. Skin was not meant to stretch that much; it looked painful and, honestly, not good.

As I handed Mary her Claritin and a drink to chug, I tried to manifest calm. I was hoping for a very rapid improvement; Mary, though, was not helping matters.

"Meg, be honest: I look like The Nutty Professor, don't I?"

To make the situation worse, Mary's speech was impaired by the swelling. The effect was reminiscent of the time my childhood next-door neighbor, Eleni, had her jaws wired shut and could only consume liquefied food through a straw.

I took a breath. I had to clench my teeth to suppress a laugh. "I mean, there is a slight Nutty Professor resemblance, but you're much, much cuter. And, hey, at least it's just a swollen lip, not a swollen everything." Then I added, to soften the blow, "You love Eddie Murphy, Mare!"

I thought Mary might have one of her Jesus moments; instead, the room filled with her trademark cackle, unhindered by the swollen mess of her lips. I couldn't help but laugh at Mary's laugh and how ludicrous the situation was. Before long, we were both laughing so hard that we had tears in our eyes.

We devoted the rest of the night to a *Clueless* and *Friday* double feature on our couch. For a while in our first year on Swinburne Street, we watched one or both every night we didn't have plans. To really do it up, we ordered a pizza for four dollars from The O on Forbes Avenue.

Mary's lips, thankfully, were not permanently misshapen. And, over time, the extreme allergic reactions became less and less frequent until they disappeared altogether. We did have to call the ambulance a different day for a hive on Mary's tongue that briefly imperiled her breathing, but we laughed our way through that episode, too. Where there is laughter, there is friendship; where there is friendship, there is laughter and love.

3. "IT'S MY THING"

For some people, hair is something you do before you leave. For Mary, hair was a way of showing—and, from time to time, reinventing—who she was. Mary was an intensely expressive person, and hair was one of the ways she announced her presence to the world. Mary loved to change her appearance, to flip the script, to reimagine her look and keep people constantly guessing. She bored easily and liked to make big, bold, physical changes, and her hair was always an important starting point. Specifically, when it came to what Mary called "Black hair," I had a significant learning curve. Prior to moving in with Mary, I thought it was all just hair; Mary soon disabused me of my naivete.

Even before we moved in together, I knew that Mary was bathroom-centric as a person. She was constantly taking baths and showers and smelled, at all times, like strawberries (this was the era of Herbal Essences). Mary had a shower cap, which intrigued me, because it was one of the first examples of such a thing I'd seen in person. Mary always seemed to take quick showers, and one day, I noticed that she didn't have her own bottle of shampoo. I should have been tipped off back when I slept at Mary's parents' house in advance of an audition—Mary didn't have a curling iron, hair dryer, or "traditional" brush to loan me.

"Mare Mare," I said, my tone inquisitive and not patronizing. "When do you wash your hair?"

"Meg," she said. "I don't." Then, after a pause she continued: "I get my hair washed every couple of weeks at the salon, and they use a relaxer. That or it's Diana Ross in *The Wiz.*"

Mary explained that hair treatment for her was a process: biweekly washing, moisturizing, conditioning, and oil treatment; nightly detangling; avoiding water. That was just the start. The number of options for styling was seemingly endless: natural look, straight, braids, cornrows, woven extensions, clip-ins, wigs, endless hair colors, and the "super short" look were just some of the possibilities.

"It's my thing," Mary said about her hair.

I was not as hair-positive. Growing up, my hair was something I was known for, not always in a good way: I was "that little red-haired girl." For a long time, I hated my strawberry blonde color because it made me feel different from everyone else. Over time, I grew to embrace the redness, but the texture was something else entirely. I had fine, thin hair that looked greasy if I didn't wash it every day. There was only so much I could do with it, and, in college, that list was further reduced to "ponytail" or "top bun" because we danced three hours a day. I later went through a Molly Ringwald phase that was liberating, in a way, because it further limited the options, but I got sick of looking at myself with the same hair, day in and day out. Mary would eventually introduce me to hair extensions, but that was still a few years away.

One day, early in the morning, I was sitting at the kitchen table, eating my usual Pop Tart. Through the haze of a moderate hangover, I watched as Mary began to pack a cooler with Tupperware and various bottles from the refrigerator. She also had an overnight bag. I managed a "Huh?"

"My dad is picking me up," Mary said. "I'm going to use my parents' car to go to my cousin's house and get my hair done."

In my compromised state, this explanation seemed totally reasonable.

The day crawled past. No Mary. The sky turned the color of a wine cooler and the sun set: Still no Mary. My hangover finally cleared. It was now Sharpie black outside. Without Mary's big personality, the house felt empty and vaguely threatening; I became aware of each floorboard creak. I tried to amuse myself with television, but Saturday night was the worst night for TV. "Dr. Quinn, Medicine Woman"? No. "Cops"? My mind began to construct narratives accounting for Mary's apparent disappearance: a flat tire; a car accident; she had run away—ergo the need for cold chicken; a serial killer feigning a broken arm. This was before the days of cell phones. I kept the landline near and, at one point, got as far as dialing a "9" and a "1."

Finally, I heard the sound of someone futzing with the lock on the side door. The door swung open and there was Mary, resplendent in the dim light of our shabby chic living room, her hair done in tight box braids inspired by Janet

Jackson in "Poetic Justice." The braids extended well past her shoulders, down the middle of her back.

"Mare Mare," I said. "You look incredible!"

The truth is that I was a little bit envious that Mary had the courage and the imagination to try such a bold look. I loved the idea of "expressive" hair and wished mine could say something more than "Different day, same Megan." Still, I had no idea what could have taken so long.

"Didn't you see me packing wigs and liquor, Meg?"

"I did," I said. "Sort of. I was having a rough morning; I didn't put two and two together."

Mary hurried to the bathroom to examine her hair more closely in the mirror.

"For a Black woman," Mary said, "Getting your hair done is a whole *experience*. And these braids took the word *experience* to a whole different level."

"They're so beautiful, Mary," I said. They really were.

"They'd better be beautiful," Mary said, "for how many braiding hair packs I needed."

I learned not to worry when, periodically, Mary would vanish for a hairstyling "experience." I also learned to be prepared, each time, for a serious look reinvention along the lines of Madonna. I found these changes inspiring: If Mary had the courage to completely reboot her appearance periodically, then maybe I could take more stylistic risks, too.

Mary's hair, like her voice, set her apart and made her special. It was an education for me. Through Mary, I learned how to braid, how to burn braid ends with a lighter, how to use an overhead drier and assist with relaxers at our house. Once we were introduced to the über-talented hair genius, Kissy, we all got our hair in check.

4. "HE REALLY LIKES YOU, MEG!"

It was a rare weekend where one or the other of us was not performing, and an even rarer weekend when Mary wasn't seeing someone. We had walked to The O for pizza, fries, and Boone's Farm with no carding.[2]

Now Mary, at the time, had a literal "strut." She knew what to move and how to move it; it was a long, slow walk intended to give her audience time to take notice. The eyes of every man in the room from eighteen to sixty, and sometimes above, would be glued to Mary as she cat-walked to the beat of an unheard Aaliyah song to freshen up her purple lipstick.

Mary's suitors were never shy. Men would stop her on the street and say things like, "Hey,

[2] What is Boone's Farm? Wine? Malt liquor? We didn't care; we just knew that it was cheap as hell. Mary hated the taste of beer. Boone's tasted like rancid cherry Kool-Aid, but, after the first gulp, it was passable.

Boo, come talk to me!" For my part, my boobs were really small then (shocking, in retrospect). My ass was decent, but I had a thin, dancer's body with little body fat. I also lacked Mary's confidence. I would just kind of awkwardly back up and let the situation play out from a safe distance.

This evening at The O, an attractive man close to our age took notice of Mary and came to our table to chat. He said he was a student at another local college. He was flirting with Mary, trying to get her number.[3]

I want to take a moment to say that I never prioritized looks when it comes to men. I wanted more personality, talent, and humor; only once a person made me smile, and not merely through bold flattery, could I start to find them physically attractive.

Mary's guy had a friend with him, the classic wingman. This "friend" was easily ten or fifteen years older than us, as evidenced by the lines around his eyes. He was also missing a few important teeth, and several others were capped in gold. I could see the "friend" eyeing me up and averted my gaze to the mound of fries

[3] To call; this was well before the dawn of texting and DMing.

before me. To get my attention, he exhaled admiringly in a way that a person might at a passing Porsche convertible. He almost whistled as he talked through the gaps: "You're bfeuutifful."

It was very sweet, so, of course I said, "Aww, thank you," and feigned interest in my food. When Mary and her suitor had finalized their plans, we made a quick exit onto Forbes Ave., bathed in the blinking neon of The O.

The next day, Mary informed me that the guy she met (call him Jason) was coming over to hang out that night and watch movies. I was really happy for her. It wasn't uncommon for one of us to hang out in the kitchen while the other person entertained a "guest" in the living room, which adjoined the bedroom via a sliding partition. This was college; there was usually homework to do, and the kitchen was our regular workspace. No problem. Then the other shoe dropped: "Meg, Jason wants to bring Greg." A pause. "He really likes you, Meg!"

I didn't need to ask who Greg was. In the back of my mind, I could see his wizened face as he eyed me up and hear his tooth-challenged pronunciation of *beautiful*.

The situation was complex. On the one hand, Mary had to know that I was repelled by this person. On the other hand, I could understand that Mary had to put herself, and her interests, first. I also intuited that, if Jason and "Greg" were a package deal, the same would need to be true of Mary and me. Mary gave me her begging eyes; I responded with the classic "quiet suffering" expression, as you might before getting a flu shot or giving a pint of blood.

"Oh, c'mon, Meg; it'll be fun!" Mary pleaded.

"Only if Greg knows that I am only hanging out as friends," I said. Tell Jason to tell him I've just started seeing someone. I'm not available."

"Will do, Meg."

"NOT AVAILABLE."

The guys arrived. Greg had brought flowers—so much for Mary passing the message along—and flashed a semi-toothy grin. Jason, with all the looks and swagger, arrived empty-handed. Mary definitely took notice.

It wasn't the worst night of my life. In Greg, I made an unlikely friend, of sorts. We talked about the Steelers, theater, and growing up in Pittsburgh. He could not have been more respectful of the fact that I was "seeing someone," but made sure that, if I should find myself single at some point, I knew who to call.

Jason lasted a few dates with Mary before being "sunsetted." Mary had high expectations for men, and her date being shown up by Greg did not portend a long and happy relationship.

Though I continued, for a while, in my role as Mary's de facto wing woman, I can't recall another double date until we met our future husbands, Steve and Ryan. Still, looking back, I don't cringe very much at the evening with Greg. It was a small favor to Mary, back in the days when we were young and free and "bfeuutifful."

5. GLADYS AND "SHIT HAPPENS"

I was sitting at the kitchen table, regarding a bowl of Rice Krispies, transfixed by its song. The dull glow of goose-gray morning light roughly matched the thrum of my hangover. I was shaken out of this stupor by the sound of Mary's hurried footfalls, which traced a line from our shared bedroom, through the living room and kitchen, behind me, into the bathroom. The door slammed shut.

Roused, I spooned my cereal to achieve an even level of milk saturation and began to eat. I was mid-chew when Mary unleashed her first volley of banshee screams from the bathroom: "OH JESUS, MEG, THE WATER IS GOING EVERYWHERE!"

Since moving into our apartment, Mary and I had an adversarial relationship with our toilet.

Our landlord, a Captain Lou Albano–looking man who was intimidating, even when not being asked for plumbing assistance, had formulated the sexist and simplistic hypothesis that *we* were responsible for the apparent "blockage"—that we, as women entering our third decade, had somehow not yet learned that feminine hygiene products could not be flushed. Because the guy was someone my dad knew, we couldn't report him. Instead, we were trying to work around our little problem, which mainly meant hoping for the best, and, when necessary, using the unadorned "Pittsburgh potty" that occupied a dark corner of the basement. Sometimes you have to do what you have to do.

Another round of Mary's screams filled the apartment: "OH JESUS, TAKE ME! OH, LORD JESUS!" I pushed past my friend, who clung to my arm, and assessed the situation. The good news was that the toilet had flushed. The bad news was that what had previously been, as far as I could tell, a partial blockage, was now, apparently, *complete*: the water was pouring over the rim of the toilet, covering the bathroom floor, engulfing Mary's and my feet. To say the toilet had overflowed would be to put it mildly: this was an Old Testament–style deluge.

When we first moved in, we were introduced to our upstairs neighbor, Gladys. Our landlord's mother-in-law, Gladys, was sweet and very, very old. Straight out of Pittsburgh central casting, she was a chain smoker who always seemed to be wearing the same house dress with no bra. She was a little hard of hearing and tended to mash her words together. We loved her, not in spite of her quirks but because of them. When Mary's mom would make her famous wedding soup—seasoned to perfection, complete with Italian bread and oyster crackers, like eating a warm hug—we would bring Gladys a bowl. When we were feeling social, we would go upstairs and chat with Gladys and eat the snickerdoodles and oatmeal cookies she always seemed to have around. Gladys would reciprocate by appearing—disconcertingly, *inside* our apartment—with Tupperware containers of cookies and other gifts; once, she even appeared with a vintage seventies Hoover sweeper (vacuum) she no longer needed. At the conclusion of each visit, Gladys would bid farewell with, "Well I'm gonna go," but the four words were collapsed into two, delivered between puffs of a perpetually un-ashed cigarette, its far end dropping little gray-white chunks onto the floor of our apartment.

When Gladys entered, materializing once again with no notice, Mary and I were standing ankle-deep in tepid water, its inexorable, petite-tsunami tide of destruction now rolling into the kitchen. In one hand, she held another container full of cookies; in the other, she grasped—the way a person might carry a stuffed animal snake—what appeared to be a vacuum cleaner cozy for use with our sweeper. Made to look like Raggedy Ann, with red, yarn hair, it would have been horrifying under normal circumstances—which these were not.

Seemingly oblivious to the toilet water swamp overtaking the low grounds of the kitchen, Gladys squished over to the bathroom in her blue slippers and handed me the cookies and cozy. What could we do but smile awkwardly and thank her?

When Gladys was gone, Mary and I fell onto each other, laughing so hard we were snorting. When the laughs had died down, Mary seized the moment: "Shit happens, Meg!" The whole apartment was filled with laughs (in addition to toilet water).

The next day, I asked my dad to bring over a plunger, and Mary and I got our first basic plumbing lesson ("Get a good seal, then thrust, thrust, thrust!"). Our two years on Swinburne Street afforded myriad opportunities for us to practice. When our toilet cup would runneth over, the refrain would always be, "Gladys!"

6. "I CAN'T USE MY HANDS."

The apartment was abuzz. We were theater kids having a blast doing imitations and Fireball shots, drinking Boone's Farm, smoking pot, speaking in silly accents, and eating every snack in the apartment plus the obligatory pizza from The O. I don't remember who all was there. I know for sure it was Mary, Amy Orlandi Cannon, and E. Clayton "Clay" Cornelious.

Mary, Clay, and I were often together; we had named ourselves The Three Amigos. Clay had a car at school and would come and rescue us and take us to the mall in the suburbs. Amy was quick-witted and excellent at impressions; she always had us in stitches imitating actors from *Saturday Night Live* and various movies of the era.

Everyone was having so much fun that it took us a while to notice that Mary had gone missing. She obviously had to be somewhere in the damn apartment: There weren't that many rooms! I called her name as I walked through our kitchen and past the divider into our room. I even went out into the yard and circled around from the outside. Finally, I made my way back to the bathroom, where I should have started, and found the door locked. I knocked. "Mare, you good?"

A series of clicks and squeaks drew my attention to the doorknob, which Mary seemed to be trying to turn. Through the door, Mary sounded befuddled: "Meg, help me. My hands won't open the door. Did we change the doorknob?"

"Um, no, Mare. It's just a regular doorknob. You just need to turn it. Maybe press the button next to it first."

No sound from the other side of the door.

I was laughing at first, and so were the other celebrants, who had gathered to see what predicament Mary had gotten herself into this time. We were well into the evening, and it was an amusing situation: Mary was stuck in the bathroom because she couldn't unlock the door and turn the knob.

As Mary's voice grew more desperate, the gravity of the situation became apparent: "Meg,

I CAN'T USE MY HANDS! I'M TRAPPED! PLEASE SAVE ME!"

I need to pause the story here and talk about the unpredictable effects of weed back in the day. This was before there were medical marijuana cards and dispensaries. Whatever you got, usually through a friend or a sketchy friend of a friend, was what you got. Throw in some Boone's Farm and a few Fireball shots (who was counting?) and it was totally plausible that Mary had, in fact, forgotten how to use her hands. But who could say? Maybe, as the result of some sudden, irreversible breakdown of motor coordination, Mary's hands would be permanently paralyzed, her fingers and thumbs useless appendages dangling pathetically at her sides. I pictured Mary living out the rest of her life in the small bathroom with the temperamental toilet. One way or another, she would have the water part covered, but how would we be able to provide her with life-sustaining food?

One by one, the party guests and I tried to coach Mary, step by step, through the process of opening the door: "Uh, Mare, you take the knob in your hand, then you kind of squeeze it and, as you're squeezing it, turn it to the right!" Nothing.

Clay, Amy, and I huddled up. The bathroom had a small, shoulder-level window that faced the side of the house. Technically, it was accessible from the outside, if the window was open and unlocked.

The plan was for Clay to put me on his shoulders, for me to push the window open, climb through, and save Mary. Amy would provide moral support.

Though I could not have passed a field sobriety test, I had a few things going for me. I was young; I was being forced to dance every day—"You've got big dreams! You want fame! Well, fame *costs*!"—along with performing, plus the long walk from the Downtown bus stop to my job at Station Square. I lived on pizza and ramen noodles, had size B (maybe) breasts, and weighed in the range of a hundred pounds. (These days, I couldn't squeeze one boob through that small-ass window.)

Things started off well enough. I managed to slide open the window and shimmy the first half of my body through. The problem was with actually descending into the bathroom: there was nothing to hold onto or break my fall. I would just have to drop like one of the sandbags used to open the curtains at the playhouse onto the pale blue tile floor below.

With Clay and Amy directing me from outside, fueled by liquid courage and adrenaline, I managed to angle myself to essentially do a handstand to get in.

As I stood up and dusted myself off, Mary gave me the closest thing she could to a hero's welcome: "Wow, Meg." My friend draped over my shoulder, I triumphantly unlocked the door and turned the knob, which worked just fine.

We were out, but Mary was struggling to stay upright. A kitchen chair wouldn't do the job; I needed to get her to bed.

Amy and Clay appeared, back inside. Amy didn't blink: "Megan, do you need a HAND?"

I couldn't laugh—yet.

The three of us got Mary to the bedroom, where we gave her the TLC she needed to float comfortably off to sleep, our angel.

8. "I DON'T SNORE"

It was the night before an important audition, and I knew that I really needed a good night's sleep. Things had started off well, but a gnawing anxiety woke me up. I then found myself fixated on the irregular rhythms and volumes of Mary's snoring.

Mary and I shared a bedroom. Though it wasn't ideal, most of the time the arrangement wasn't a problem. Mary and I were both from big families and we were used to someone being around. It wasn't like Mary took up a lot of space: though she was brassy through and through, Mary was physically tiny. Also, Mary had an endearing, childlike side. If she had a bad date, was stressed about a test, or wasn't feeling well, she would bring her pillow and blanket over to my bed and say, "Meg, I need a friend. Move over," and spend the rest of the night on my bed. We would talk for hours—laughing, crying, telling stories, trading words of wisdom—until, finally, one or the other of us would fall silent and sleep would take over.

If questioned, Mary would always flatly deny that she *ever* snored, but the truth is that she was a back-sleeper who "sawed logs" most of the night, every night. Mary's snores were like kittens in that no two were exactly alike, ranging from a cute, soft, nasally whisper—think of kittens sleeping piled on top of one another—to more guttural, at times alarmingly loud, snorts. Before going to bed, I would always include this prayer: "Please, God, let me fall asleep before Mare starts snoring. Please."

On this particular night, I became focused on the snores, which seemed to take on an almost mocking tenor. As with Vecna from "Stranger Things" before an attack covered in slime, each series of snores would start off quietly, only to build into a terrible, grunted crescendo.

I tried everything: covering my head with a pillow, elevating Mary's head, turning her on her left side, nudging her to wake her up long enough to buy myself some time to sleep. Nothing was working, and, before long, I was starting to wig out. Sleep is such a basic need and, when it is denied to you for reasons beyond your control, you begin the descent into meltdown territory.

I grabbed my pillow, comforter, and Hamlet, my stuffed pig, and "jiggled" open the roll-out vinyl divider—the sort of thing that separates viewing rooms at funeral homes—that partitioned our bedroom from the living room. Sleeping necessities in hand, I deposited myself, with considerable relief, onto the couch: Finally, I was going to get some rest.

Then, I felt something move. A body. I started and turned to find a semi-blanketed figure, eyes closed, corpse-like in red-black Pittsburgh witching hour light. It took me a few seconds to work it out: good-looking man of color, our couch, telltale paper bag on the coffee table. The sleep-deprived neurons in my brain made the connection—Mary's new boyfriend, Shawn! He had pretty much taken a bus to our apartment one day and never left, except to go out at night. He must have gotten "home" late; it was actually kind of sweet that he'd slept on the couch.

Unfortunately, I was now wide awake with nowhere to go. I briefly considered my options—kitchen floor, my favorite bench outside—before concluding that the only workable possibility was the living room floor. I shaped my blanket into a kind of nest; roosted, birdlike, into my creation; and tried to salvage what sleep I could.

The next morning, I was eating a Pop Tart at the kitchen table when Mary and Shawn entered the room. Mary was bemused: "Meg, why did you sleep . . . on the floor?"

Mary's words echoed through the headache gray of my mind. I wasn't even mad; I was exhausted. "The snoring, Mary," I said. "It was just too much."

Mary erupted into a peal of her trademark cackle. "Meg, I don't snore."

Resistance was futile. I took a bite of Pop Tart and tried to bring myself to a place of unconditional love.

9. "MY EYE — OUCH OUCH!!!!"

One night, I returned home from a party on Halket Street to find Mary and Shawn having a picnic on our living room floor, with a blanket set up with a candle, an array of snacks and cheeses, and two champagne flutes (a significant upgrade over our usual pizza squares). The two seemed to be having a great night, and I was happy for them. I brushed my teeth, then maneuvered around the happy couple to the bedroom, worked the divider shut, and flipped on *Saturday Night Live* at a relatively high volume.

Mary and I were in the prime of our dating lives, but we had different approaches. Whereas Mary usually had a boyfriend of some sort, I was a serial dater who "didn't like labels." I have a godawful lack of direction, so, with every new date, I would hand Mary the phone and ask her to explain to the prospective bachelor how to get to our place. This would also serve as a kind of screening process.

Mary and I were protective of one another. We had opened up our pasts: the trials, tribulations, and traumas. We were so close that anyone lucky enough to enter the inner circle was always being watched, just in case.

At the end of a date night, Mary would be waiting for me, and I would typically say, “Nope, he wore a pink shirt,” or “He was too cocky,” “More of a friend,” or “Even though he was going to be a doctor, he didn’t get my heart pumping.” The truth was that I had a fear of commitment and feeling tied down; I was living my best life and wasn’t ready for the narrative to change.

At the time, Mary was dating Shawn. Shawn took care of himself and dressed well. He was over a foot taller than Mary, but the height difference was mitigated by Mary’s affinity for the highest of heels. Though Shawn had a warm disposition and seemed smart—Mary had a low tolerance for fools—he came with a few red flags. Red flag #1: He seldom left our apartment. Red flag #2: Though Shawn would never show us his license, he looked approximately ten years older than us. #3: He would never show us his license. It was possible he didn’t have one, but either way, his caginess about the issue felt strange. #4: He never seemed to have any money. In fairness to Shawn, neither did we, but we were undergrad fine arts majors. If Shawn had been in law school, or whatever, the lack of funds wouldn't have been worrying, but we never really knew for sure what, or whether, Shawn was studying. Finally, red flag #5: On the rare occasion that Shawn spent some time away, he would show up carrying his extra clothes and toiletries in a brown paper bag.

Mary and Shawn had skipped the dating stage and made a beeline straight into acting like a married couple. It isn't exaggerating to say that they met one night, hit it off, and then Shawn showed up at our door, paper bag in hand. He was around our place so much that I came to see him as a permanent fixture, not unlike the divider between the living room and bedroom that was so often in place when he was over. Still, I know how to get along with people, and Shawn and I had become friends, almost cousins, along the lines of Scooby and Scooby-Dum.

It had been an auspicious beginning for Mary and Shawn, but recently, perhaps because he literally resided at our apartment, Mary had begun to cool on her "boo." Whereas, at first, when Mary spoke of him, *Shawn* had been illuminated with neon, now the name was illuminated by a single flickering light bulb, if it was lit at all. Worse, the two lovebirds had begun to bicker and go after each other like George and Louise Jefferson—not a promising sign for a new couple. It would be a long goodbye, and not without its fireworks. As Mary's bestie, I was on guard.

Anyway, there I was on my bed, semi-dozing, watching *SNL*. It was a transitional year: Molly Shannon and Will Ferrell were still new and trying to find their comedic footing. At some point, the soft pitter-patter of conversation between Mary and Shawn from the other side of the divider was interrupted by a loud shriek from Mary: "My eye—ouch, ouch!!!"

For reasons that, in retrospect, I can't quite pinpoint, Mary's voice shot through me like a bee sting. I found myself on my feet, my fight or flight response fully engaged.

Heart pounding, I yanked the divider open and bounded into the living room. Mary was on her knees, covering her eye. Like a crazed mother spider monkey defending its infant from a hungry ocelot, I threw myself onto

Shawn's back and latched on with both hands. Though Shawn was much bigger than I was, I had the advantages of surprise and unending hours of torturous *Fame*-level dance classes under my belt. Shawn stood up and tried to shake me off, but still I clung, fingernails digging into his shoulder. "CALL 911!" I panted. "Now!"

"Meg, Meg, STOP!" Mary pleaded. "STOP! HE DIDN'T PUNCH ME. I GOT CHAMPAGNE IN MY CONTACT LENS!"

On the word "LENS," I released my grip and dropped from the six feet or so off Shawn's back to the carpeted floor, inert.

We were all basically fine. I had broken a nail; Mary had to wear her dreaded glasses (which Shawn had already seen plenty of); and Shawn now saw me, not inaccurately, as someone a beat away from launching an unhinged physical assault. I was okay with this: it's not like he was without question marks.

Shawn graciously accepted my apology—he understood that the situation looked bad and that Mary was my best friend. Shawn suggested that we order two "O" pizzas. Because at least two of us were in college, that made total sense, fast approaching past midnight on a Sunday morning. Except: *Why* two *pizzas?*

"Oh," Shawn explained, "Don't worry, I can eat the leftovers."

10. A FLYING CHAIR

Early one Saturday afternoon, I came home after a date with Steve. Everything was locked tight, and Mary was not answering my frantic knocks. Finally, I dug around my purse, found my keys, and let myself in. I knew a fight was coming: It had been brewing for a long time.

Officially, Steve and I first met at the bus stop. I was going to Point Park and he was headed to Duquesne University, where he was a senior biology major. Steve and I had gone to the same high school, Thomas Jefferson, where he had been a year ahead of me. Everyone at TJ knew who Steve was: he was the "nice" football player and half of one of the more conspicuous couples in the school. His then-girlfriend, Amy Vogel-Frantz, was an actor and friend of mine. She and Steve were glued at the hip—though Amy later broke things off, sometime after enrolling as a musical theater major at Point Park.

As we waited for the bus, Steve was charming and made conversation. Whereas some guys I had met had been cold or distant, Steve was engaging, with blue eyes and an easy smile. When he asked me for my number, I was wary of the Amy connection: that very morning, I was on my way to the Playhouse to rehearse a scene with her. Only after getting Mary's permission did I consent to go to a party at his house. He urged me to "bring friends," and I did. Only later did I learn that he told his million roommates, "The redhead is mine." Things progressed from there.

Mary had been off and on with Shawn for months, and they were currently off. For the first time in our friendship, Mary and I had switched places: she was single, and I was seeing someone. Mary had always been protective of me and of our friendship, and she was deeply suspicious of anyone who came into our little bubble. Initially, she was dismissive of Steve because he wasn't one of our mutual friends. He didn't have much in common with two actors, and I think she felt he was stealing me from her. I struggled to balance both relationships, which were equally important to me, and to give everyone equal time.

I didn't want to make Mary feel uncomfortable by bringing Steve around all the time. As much as I loved Mary, when Shawn basically moved in, it was awkward at times for me to be home. For that reason, I would hang at Steve's place more often than not. Mary responded by going into lockdown, both literally and emotionally. She would never acknowledge, much less talk about, my relationship with Steve. It was brutal.

Finally, on a bus ride together to Point Park, Mary broached the subject: "Meg, just so you know, Steve is not my type of person. We will never be friends. I know that may be uncomfortable for you, but it's not happening."

This just broke my heart. I couldn't imagine two people who meant everything to me not being in the same room, ever, comfortably. Naturally, I told Steve and he amped it up even more to try to joke with Mary—to get her to be on "Team Steve." One morning he showed up with breakfast from McDonald's. Mary took the Egg McMuffin he handed her, pushed the "open" pedal on the garbage can, and tossed it in.

"I already ate," the Ice Queen said.

It was awkward as hell.

So there I was, entering Fort Mary. The second I got in the door, she laid into me about Steve and my never being around. She had the gall to bring up Shawn and started comparing Steve to Shawn, a "real man." This really got to me because Shawn, though he had always been nice enough to me, had become our de facto third roommate, never had any money, never bought her (or me) food, never contributed to the chores, never drove (who knew if he even had a license), and basically treated Mary horribly. Shawn was pretty much the definition of a "scrub"; if anything, Mary deserved someone more like Steve. When I said as much, it was *on.*

You know those arguments when all the feelings you had repressed to keep waters calm come the hell out like a backed-up toilet? That was this fight.

Never one to let a jab go un-countered, Mary went straight for the jugular: "Do you know what my mother said about you the other day?!"

Now Mrs. Johnson and I were close; how could we not be when we had spent hours together on all fours, lit by klieg light, looking for Mary's damn contact? I knew that either a)

Mrs. Johnson had never actually said anything bad about me or b) She had said something benign that Mary was about to embellish to the maximum extent in order to make me feel awful.

I didn't take the bait: "No, Mare, I don't care," I said. "I love your mom. I'm not interested in this story. I don't give a rat's ass what your mom said."

Mary then changed tack, returning to the "Shawn is a real man" line of argument.

This I could not abide: "Mare, that *man* is an entitled ass with not one fucking redeemable quality!"

I felt something whoosh past my head.

When we moved in, Mary had read up on Feng shui, which apparently dictated that there needed to be sufficient seating to achieve a positive "chi." She had produced two old wooden chairs from the basement, dusted them off, and voila. One of those chairs had just been thrown across the room—not *at* me, exactly, but in my direction.

I started doing the maniacal crazy laugh I had learned from my dad, a champion yeller in his heyday, whose argument toolkit was vast and deep. "Mare, this is crazy," I said. "I love you, but

I don't have to live here like this. I will just move back to the dorms, or move home and commute. I don't need this."

The room was as silent as the "house" in a theater in the millisecond between the lights going down and the curtains going up. In a way, the curtain *was* going up—on a new era of my friendship with Mary, though the script had yet to be written.

Two-and-a-half years of training and performance had only served to sharpen Mary's natural flair for drama. She slowly made her way across the room, returned the chair to its wooden legs, and sat on it, facing me.

Another moment of silence ensued. Then, almost as an act of God, the damaged chair legs buckled and collapsed, sending Mary to the floor with a crash. I hurried over to help my friend, surrounded by shards of chair, up to her feet—only to slip and fall onto the floor next to her.

I can't recall who broke character first, and it doesn't matter. Laughter filled the room, and we hugged each other tight; our bond was restored.

As with many fights, mine with Mary wasn't about what we had thought. As their years of friendship would later prove, Mary had no reason to hate Steve. She had just never let him into her heart and given him a chance. Mary was simply missing me and our bond as kindred spirits. I had felt the same thing when Shawn showed up with his paper bag.

It was just like in the TV adaptation of *Anne of the Island* when Anne says, of her best friend Diana's fiancé, Fred, "He had no business waltzing in and stealing my best friend."

Mary didn't immediately stop feeling uneasy or being protective, but she accepted my choice of a boyfriend, and later husband. Because she loved me, she didn't make me choose.

11. THE SEXY GLAMOUR PARTY

As the second half of junior year was winding down, Mary and I decided we wanted to have a big "theme party" for all of our theater peers and friends at Point Park. Plumbing issues notwithstanding, we had a great apartment, and we were eager to share the wealth.

Our theme brainstorm didn't take much time: "glamour" was the obvious way to go. We chose a date and spread the word, which then spread itself. In the buildup to the party, everyone put time, imagination, and whatever money they had into perfecting their outfits—people were going *in*.

I remember that Mary settled on something very clingy; she had the best, muscle-defined Tina Turner legs, and I always loved when she wore skirts or dresses that showed off her strut. For my part, I wore a long, red, evening gown with a long slit up one of the legs; in fact, it was a hand-me-up from my little sister Katie, something she had worn to a formal dance in high school. A pair of sexy, red stilettos completed the outfit.

Steve offered to lend a hand with bouncing duties as necessary. Shawn, with whom Mary was back *on*, graciously offered to make us yucca punch, which, I imagined, would add an exotic, desert edge to the proceedings.

We divided the basement into three different bar stations. Mary, who hated cigarette smoke, had the idea of setting aside a designated smoking section. We weren't sure what to do with the decidedly unglamorous Pittsburgh potty in the corner. Mary hung a fancy, frilly curtain around the commode with the idea that the added privacy and flair would encourage people to use it; given our recent "Gladys" overflow situation, we were reluctant to use the upstairs toilet too much.

Before long, the party was crowded with glammed-up Point Park students, their friends, a smattering of Steve's Duquesne friends, and random strangers off the street. Each of the three bars was manned by a different, volunteer partygoer. Almost everyone danced. Steve kept his eye on the few random creepers and helped do noise control. The whole room was thick with cigarette smoke. (Everyone seemed to be baffled by the potty behind the country-cute shower curtain.)

As the party was reaching its peak, through the haze of smoke, Shawn appeared. Sans trademark paper bag, he carried two paint buckets containing "yucca punch": jug-grade vodka, fruit juice, sliced lemons and limes, and half-melted ice. This was not exactly the height of glamour, but by then, no one was in any condition to judge.

You know it's a successful party when a random partygoer falls on your kitchen floor, shouts, "THIS IS THE BEST FUCKING PARTY EVER!" and promptly pees his pants.

I can still hear Mary laughing—or was it screaming? It was quite a night.

12. SUNDAY SPRING CLEANS WITH ARETHA

I remember Mary broaching the topic midweek over our family dinner of ramen noodles: "Meg, it's spring. This Saturday we need to wake up early, like 6 a.m., and deep clean our place. It's fucking gross in here."

I chewed my fork full of noodles and slow-blinked. Normally, my weekend morning plans included one or more of the following: sleeping, eating Pop Tarts, hanging out with Steve, binge-watching episodes of *The Real World* or *Road Rules*, and maybe, depending on my level of ambition, doing homework or learning a new song for school. Waking up at "like 6 a.m." to "deep clean" was not on the menu.

In the Johnson family, seasonal family "cleanings" were a tradition. Every person would pitch in. Couches and kitchen appliances would be moved, floors would be vacuumed, swept, and mopped, surfaces would be dusted, walls would be washed down (a new one to me). Mary herself had always been very clean. Her closet was immaculate, her clothes organized into a color "rainbow." She couldn't leave dishes in the sink. Our apartment didn't have a dishwasher, but Mary claimed that she would have hand washed the dishes even if it did: "I don't trust it," she said of a dishwasher. "Hand wash is better!"

There was no equivalent tradition in my family. Occasionally, the kids had been sent down to the game room to put the toys in boxes. My older sister Jenny would climb up on the couch, declare herself the supervisor, and boss my brother Stephen, little sister Katie, and me around like a trio of scruffy kids in a Victorian workhouse. Personally, I was relatively neat on the surface—just as long as you didn't open a drawer or closet.

Back at family dinner, Mary was pure enthusiasm: "We can clean to music, Meg! We can move the furniture together and really get into the corners. It'll be like a fresh start!"

It was decided.

When, Saturday at 6 a.m., our alarms went off, it felt like a joke—but Mary could not have been more serious. After a quick breakfast, Mary wrapped her hair in an old scarf and gave me a bandanna for my strawberry blonde bob.

"What is this, Halloween?" I protested.

"You're wearing it today," Mary said.

Mary produced latex gloves from under the sink. She filled our lone bucket with hot, soapy water. We began with the kitchen: two fine arts majors dragging the refrigerator away from the wall—*Who knew it had wheels?*—and even moving the oven (I was afraid we were going to blow up the house). We dusted the countertops, then swept, then scrubbed everything: counters, the exteriors of cabinets, the damn *walls*, and finally the floor. By the time we were finished, the linoleum kitchen floor glimmered with a cartoon sparkle.

"That wasn't so bad," I said, admiring our work.

"That was just the first room, Meg," Mary said.

It was late enough now that Mary had no qualms about blasting music. She hit play on *The Very Best of Aretha Franklin, Volume 1* and cranked our boombox. As we tackled the bathroom, Mary belted out each song along with Lady Soul, their voices commingling in the tiled space into a single, sublime whole. From Aretha, we moved on to the Fugees—we both loved Lauryn Hill, Toni Braxton, and even a little Shaggy with "It Wasn't Me." After we had scrubbed the living room walls, Mary decided, once again, to try to hone the room's feng shui. After rearranging everything, we agreed we hated it and dragged all the furniture back to its original position.

The bedroom came last. This was where, I'll admit, my little clutter problem was most pronounced. Mary was uncompromising: if I didn't love it or need it, it was gone.

In the end, we celebrated with an "O" pizza, bottles of Boones, and a rewatching of *Clueless*, of which we both knew every word. We were asleep by ten at the latest.

At the end of our second lease, when our landlord claimed that we weren't getting our security deposit back because he needed to hire a cleaner, we had to laugh. No professional could have been more thorough than we were under Mary's watchful eye, powered by Aretha Franklin and our friendship.

ACT 2: SISTER ACT

1. BONAPARTE, REXINGTON, AND THE HUGE-ASS DINOSAUR VAN

It was fall 1997. That spring, Mary and I had graduated from Point Park. We were still in that semi-limbo space where we were considering moving to New York and starting to audition, to give our degrees a shot in the big, bad, real world. We were living with our families. I was dating Steve pretty seriously, and Mary was starting to date Ryan.

We were trying to start earning money as professional actresses, even if we had to stay local. We accepted roles in back-to-back theater productions at the Peasant Village Dinner Theater in Rostraver to get practice in, build our experience, and make a bit of money. Meanwhile, we were checking want ads in the back of the paper for paid acting gigs that were daylight and local.

When I found an ad for children's theater actors, I thought I had struck gold. We were hired to present a traveling show about fossils and dinosaurs for the Carnegie Museum of Natural History. Mary and I would play paleontologists. I would be "Professor Bonaparte," Mary would be "Dr. T. Rexington." We would visit schools in Western Pennsylvania, West Virginia, and Eastern Ohio. The pay was respectable. Neither of us knew the first thing about paleontology, but we would be given a resource book to study and bring with us on school visits. The catch was we would have to do everything ourselves: the rehearsing, the driving, the building and taking down of the set at each location. We chose to look on the bright side: against all odds, we were employed, traveling actresses.

I was blessed that Mary had a fantastic sense of direction. She felt very powerful driving a huge van with a T. rex picture on one side and a brontosaurus on the other. If you know me, you know I can barely drive my own car; the idea of me behind the wheel of a massive van was almost comical, and I was happy to cede that responsibility to Mary.

Though the show was successful, it was also a huge test of our friendship. We spent most of our eight-hour days traveling and performing together in school cafegymatoriums. Nights were spent at local theaters rehearsing and performing together. It was a theater marriage.

One day, Mary wanted to challenge me, or maybe make a point—or maybe she was just tired.

"Meg," she announced. "You need to drive the van tomorrow and get some practice in."

I couldn't argue with her. It was clearly my turn, and if my best friend and costar wanted me to step up, then I should do it, right? The problem was that, of all mornings for me to "step up," Mary picked one in which we were supposed to drive somewhere in Ohio.

That night I barely slept. I woke up an hour early saying to myself, "Well, Meg, you had a nice run, maybe not a long one, but a good one. You are most likely going to either get lost in the van today or crash and die on impact."

On the road, I tried to project calm. The first part of the trip went okay. It wasn't until I took a very wide turn—the unfortunate motorcyclist must have seen his life flash before his eyes—

that Mary volunteered to drive the rest of the way there.

We got to the school and, as usual, had to assemble a plant-eating dinosaur and a huge projector. The whole show was based on a corny slide show. The screen was huge and clunky and a pain in the ass to assemble.

Mary noticed that the school already had a screen set up. "Fuck it, Meg," she said. "We are using that screen!"

After taking our break before the show and putting on our safari hats, a problem became apparent. When we tried a slide or two as a dry run, we couldn't help but notice that the projected images were not only the size of a postage stamp but were literally backward and upside down.

A chill ran up and down my spine.

Mary, though, was insistent: "We don't have time to set up the other screen, Meg. We won't be able to use the slides."

The essence of Mary's words appeared in a bubble floating over my head: NO SLIDES. Ever so gently, I tried to protest: "Ummm, Mare, the thing is . . . the whole show is told through those slides."

Tired from the drive, Mary did not feel like rushing to assemble the screen: "We can just *describe* the slides and they can imagine it. That's what kids do! It's fucking fine, Meg."

Through a combination of my own stubbornness and kid-glove persuasion, I was finally able to convince Mary to help me put up the correct screen. Though she had grudgingly taken the loss, she was barely able to hide her resentment throughout the show: The playfulness of our characters was, on this day, very much acting.

Every day, at the end of our performance, we were supposed to answer questions from audience members. As neither of us had spent any time studying the resource book, we both secretly prayed there would be no questions, or just easy ones. We only knew the script.

On this day, just as the Q&A portion was ending, a bespectacled student raised his hand.

"The young man in the front," I said, and hoped for a softball question.

"Did birds come from dinosaurs?"

In the late nineties, we had still just come around to depicting dinosaurs with raised tails. Most of what I knew about dinosaurs came from Land of the Lost. I hadn't yet gotten the memo about chickens being direct descendants of theropods.

I tried to buy time: "I didn't quite get that, hun. Can you repeat the question?"

"Are birds dinosaurs?"

Straining to maintain a stilted grin, I kicked the question around my head. Were birds dinosaurs? If so, that was news to me. Everyone knew that dinosaurs were extinct and that birds were, well, birds. So that seemed to cover it, right? But what if the kid knew something I didn't? What if, all along, birds *had* been dinosaurs and dinosaurs weren't really extinct? I mean, if you thought about it, bird feed did kind of look like dinosaur feet. T. rex walked on two feet and so did birds. Also, damn, pterodactyls could fly. Dinosaurs, though, didn't have feathers—plus dinosaurs were extinct. Fuck!

I stared blankly in the hope that Mary would improvise some kind of semi-suitable answer. Mary, however, was nowhere to be seen. As my eyes scanned for my costar, I tried to stall: "That's a really interesting question. Are birds—which we see every day, all around us, flying around, eating at bird feeders, sometimes pooping on us—are birds dinosaurs?"

At last, from behind the original screen, Mary emerged.

"I'm going to turn this one over to my colleague, Dr. Rexington," I said.

A model of coolness, Mary assumed an almost professorial mien: "*Archaeopteryx*," Mary said. "It had feathers like a bird, but the teeth and tail of a dinosaur. It was kind of like a hybrid. Scientists theorize, based on this, that birds may have evolved from dinosaurs, with Archaeopteryx being an important link in the chain."

I glanced at my friend with a combination of bafflement and awe. Where the heck did *that* come from?

Later, as the kids were being led out of the room, I said to Mary under my breath: "Nice work, Dr. Rexington. How the hell did you come up with *that*?"

"Wouldn't you like to know?" Mary said.

As we were taking down the set, I noticed a textbook open on the ground a ways back. And there was my answer: *The damn resource book.*

What I couldn't understand was how Mary had managed to pronounce "Archaeopteryx" correctly.

"Did I pronounce it correctly, Meg?" Mary said.

We laughed so hard, and for so long, that the drive almost felt short. Mary drove without complaint.

2. CINNABON

As shows at the Peasant Village Dinner Theater and the dinosaur van gigs were not exactly lucrative, Mary and I were forced to supplement our incomes with part-time jobs at Century III Mall. I was working at American Eagle Outfitters and Mary was waitressing at Ruby Tuesday, where my sister Jenny worked as a hostess. Most days, the three of us could carpool in "Franny," my very old, refurbished Mercury Cougar that Steve's dad had restored for me for free. When our schedules allowed, we would lunch together at the food court.

A few stores down from American Eagle was a Cinnabon. The sickly-sweet smell of huge cinnamon rolls permeated the air in my part of the mall. As I was an avowed "spicy food" person (I joked that if you deep-fried a tennis shoe and added some spice, I would eat it), the aroma had no effect on me, other than making me mildly

nauseated. Mary, though, had a sweet tooth, and whenever she would drop by my store, she would find herself following the Cinnabon scent to its source. Mary couldn't get over the fact that there was only one food item on the menu: "It's a Cinnabon or nothing, Meg! It's almost zen!"

On one of her Cinnabon stops, Mary discovered that a friend of hers from Elizabeth Forward High School was one of the managers of the store. Mary had a way of charming everyone, so it came as little surprise to me when Mary appeared in American Eagle boasting that her manager friend had given her a Cinnabon free of charge.

An occasional gooey cinnamon role is, for those so disposed, a guilty pleasure: no harm done. For Mary, though, these free Cinnabons became an almost daily, prework ritual, with an occasional, supplemental, midday "pick-me-up" not out of the question.

One day, over shared chicken fingers in the food court, Mary seemed uncomfortable in her Ruby Tuesday server getup, contorting herself and extending her arms and legs to find more room in her clothes.

I gave her side-eye.

"Honestly, Meg, what the shit? Everything is tight! I'm not doing anything different!"

Though I felt uncomfortable broaching the subject, I had no choice: "Uh, Mare, what about all the Cinnabons?"

Mary was indignant: "Nah, other than that, I barely eat, Meg! And I get tons of exercise: I walk all over the mall, dance at rehearsals, do the stupid toe-touches your dad taught us."

A couple days later, I was getting breakfast at the food court before work. Mary ordered a bagel with low-fat cream cheese. I raised my eyebrows: "What about your free Cinnabon?"

Mary lowered her gaze. "My friend cut me off. She said she was concerned about my health."

I couldn't contain my laughter. "You can still pay for them, Mare," I said when I could manage speech.

Mary gave me side-eye.

"Are you still going to visit me?" I said.

"Don't even, Meg," Mary said.

"It's okay, Mary," I said. "You can always luxuriate in the Cinnabon smell."

"Oh no," Mary said. "The smell!" She let out a series of stage sobs.

We ate at our usual table by the rail overlooking the ramp to Lazarus. When we were finished, we went back to our crummy-ass, part-time jobs. If, in the post-Cinnabon era, Mary's job seemed crummier, she didn't let on.

3. SING THE SONG AND FIX THE DRESS

I trusted Mary with my life, so of course I entrusted her with keeping my wedding day, October 23, 1999, on schedule. Admittedly, I had some reservations. It wasn't so much that Mary was always late, though she was; it was that Mary had her own sense of time. Part of being friends with Mary was accepting she would get there when she got there, and having trust that everything was usually going to be okay.

I had gotten off to a late start myself. I slept at my parents' house in Pleasant Hills and woke up early for the obligatory "breakfast with my dad" (the undisputed king of Quaker Oats; they should seriously dress him up in period garb and put his face on the box). Next, I drove to the beautician. My veil was a ring of tiny roses that would require a full bun to "fill in" the circle. At the "hair trial day," I had worked with a stylist named Melissa and all had gone well: the look evoked *Anne of Avonlea* without being cloyingly vintage. When we arrived at the salon, however, Melissa was nowhere to be seen.

"I'm here for my wedding hair appointment?" I said, presenting the statement as a question. "I had a trial with Melissa a few weeks ago."

"Oh *Melissa*," a hairdresser I had never seen before said, approaching. "You must be Megan?"

I nodded.

"Melissa is on a planned trip to Iceland," the stylist said. "My name is Nicole, and I'm going to be doing your styling today."

All the blood drained from my face.

"Don't worry, hun," the stylist said. "I spoke to Melissa and I know what the plan is." She leafed through a kind of Rolodex and produced a cropped sheet of paper. "We're going to be doing a *bun* today; is that right?"

Whatever Melissa had done to get my fine hair to fill out the "circle" of my veil was either not communicated, not understood, or no longer physically possible. Or maybe Nicole just lacked Melissa's touch. Whatever the case, the original hair design was a literal flop. Mortified, I watched as Nicole tried with increasing desperation to improvise a solution. When I finally left the salon, fighting back tears, I was running at least fifteen minutes late.

Entering the house, I could hear peals of laughter coming from the dining room. I was touched that the bridal party—my sisters Jenny and Katie, my sister-in-law Tammy Schmidt, friends Nique Eagen, Priscilla Rodd, and Crickett Householder, with Mary as maid of honor—was really gelling. I rounded the corner into the dining room only to find my "girl squad" in sweats, grazing from the lunchmeat, veggies, and German potato salad arrayed on the table. At the head was Mary, ever the "belle of the ball," even in yoga pants, holding court.

"MEGAN," the bridesmaids said, greeting me warmly with hugs. "YOU LOOK SO BEAUTIFUL."

I tried to fake a smile and reciprocate the love, but I had some questions. Mary beat me to the punch.

"I just got here, Meg!" she said.

"Um, Mare," I said. "Nobody is dressed. *I'm* not dressed. My hair needs to be redone and the photographer is going to be here in twenty minutes!"

At that moment, perfectly on cue, the doorbell rang. I could hear my mom greeting the photographer, guiding her the ten paces to the dining room.

"The photographer's here," my mom announced. A youngish woman draped in cameras waved sheepishly.

A long couple of seconds passed in silence.

"Wow," my mom said in her monotone voice. "No one is dressed!" Then, circling me, scrutinizing the stylist's work, running her fingers along the edges of my hair: "You look pretty, Mo, but your veil and hair don't look like the picture. Your bun isn't filling the ring; it seems flat. We need to fix it."

"I know, mum," I snipped.

Once again, I could feel the tears welling up in my hazel eyes. I was saved by an echoey voice in the dark corner of my mind that was clinging to rationality: "*Meg, no! Your makeup!*"

Mary stepped forth: "Meg, don't worry, we got this!" Then, to the photographer. "Hi, I'm Mary, I'm the maid of honor. What's your name?"

"Martha," the photographer said.

"Great to meet you, Martha," Mary said. "I'm sure you're going to do a great job today. Look, you're early, right?"

"I like to arrive early just to—" Martha began.

Mary cut her off: "Look, we're gonna need at least ten minutes just to get everyone looking tip top. There's plenty to eat here. Just grab some lunch—the potato salad is great!"

Mary then turned to the rest of the bridal party: "Ladies, let's throw on our gowns and help Meg get into her dress." Then: "Who here is good with hair?" Priscilla and my sister Jenny raised their hands. "Great. Priscilla and Jenny, once Megan is dressed, can you concentrate on the hair?"

It was agreed.

Everyone was dressed in record time and the bridesmaids showed great care in turning me into a princess. Despite everyone's best efforts to salvage the bun, my hair remains my one regret in the pictures. When it became clear that the look wasn't going to take, my gut feeling had been to change tacks completely—go with a different veil and a different look, my hair down and curly. Alas, there was neither the time nor the "Melissa."

We took a bazillion pics, and all the ladies loaded into the stretch limo for champagne and strawberries. As we crossed the sidewalk into the cavernous Saint Thomas à Becket Roman Catholic Church, now Triumph of the Holy Cross, anticipation and snow flurries filled the air.

There was a scramble to locate the ring and ring pillow that my poor cousin, David, needed to fulfill his duties. "How can I be 'ring boy' without a ring?" he pleaded. But both were found after only a mild panic.

The ceremony was gorgeous, a little cold, and very long and Catholic—I was very fortunate to be wearing gloves.

Steve cried when he saw me in my dress.

Though it had not been the plan, both of my parents gave me away, one on each arm. As we walked, Mary sang a stunning rendition of "Ave Maria."

When Steve and I were both at the altar, Mary hurried over to fix my dress.

The officiant, Father Bob, quipped, "Wow! The music, fixing the dress. The maid of honor is working up a sweat!"

Of course, it was too frigid in the sanctuary for anyone to work up a sweat.

Though it was Father Bob's first wedding ceremony, it went off without a hitch. No one had told Steve and me that the famous, "You may now kiss the bride" was not part of the Catholic "Rite of Marriage." After the blessing, we paused for a second, not sure what to do, then kissed without prompting.

The reception was the party and catharsis we all needed it to be. With his thinning red hair styled into a perm at Mary's request, Ryan, Steve's best man, gave a knockout speech. The food was predictably mediocre. When the toasts and rituals were over, everyone danced into the middle-evening. When the music stopped, as it does early in the suburbs of Pittsburgh, my dad slipped the reception hall manager and DJ some extra money to keep the party going. Mary, grooving in her bridesmaid's dress and Isotoner slippers, was the life of the party.

When it was all over, with the last stragglers claiming the remnants of the cookie table, Mary pulled me into her arms.

"You did it, Meg!" she whispered.

I corrected her: "*We* did it, Mare."

"Another journey started," Mary whispered.

"Another journey together," I said.

"I'll share you with Steve," she whispered. "But I'm still number one."

"Of course you are, Mare," I laughed. "I love you."

We hugged each other tighter.

4. SHOULD "OLD" ACQUAINTANCE BE FORGOT

"Guys, it's all planned," Mary declared to Steve, Ryan, and me one night over drinks.

We had been discussing something to do for New Year's Eve. Part of the problem with the sudden onset of adulthood was the loss of community. Mary and I still had actor friends, and we made new ones with each production we were in, but the numbers paled in comparison to our group at Point Park. People were more dispersed.

Our "Y2K" gathering had struck a bitter note with Mary. It had been us, Steve and Ryan, Jenny and her husband Rich, and Mary's sister Karen. We had a fine time, but the modest scene had clashed with Mary's self-image. To her, it was a disappointment. What were we doing, hanging around a house in West Mifflin at the end of the millennium? One of Mary's resolutions was that next year would be different.

As November passed into December, Mary combed the different listings looking for the kind of all-inclusive blowout that I guess she had wanted the year before. The Bradley House, the hall where my wedding reception had been held, was hosting a party with a sit-down dinner, dancing, and a complimentary champagne bottle to ring in the year. We could get dressed up, and, because it was "pay by the group," the price was right.

The guys were skeptical. Their idea of a good time was working their way through a keg of Miller Light and talking about the Steelers. If my soon-to-be brother-in-law, Rich, really wanted to party, he'd bring a bottle of Goldschläger schnapps. That was how they rolled.

"Listen," Mary said. "Let's compromise. Let's do the Bradley House—hell, it's *cheap* when you break it down by person—then we can go to one of our houses and have an after-party. That way everyone gets what they want."

To me, the obvious problem with this was that none of us would be in a condition to have an "after-party," but Mare was so excited and adorable—and it was hard to resist an excited

Mary. I reluctantly agreed, and everyone else fell into line.

The big night arrived. It was me and Steve, Mare and Ry, and Jenny and Rich. As usual, the ladies took time and effort planning their attire. The guys reluctantly wore ties.

About two seconds after arrival, it was apparent that we were the youngest party goers at the event by a good thirty years. The music was early jazz and big band stuff (think "Boogie Boogie Bugle Boy") clearly targeted at the "Greatest Generation," which had come out in force. White-haired men and women attempted to swing dance. All that was missing was a bingo table and an early-bird special.

The sit-down dinner was as expected: moderately fresh rolls and squares of butter; iceberg lettuce salad, etc. The "Amish" chicken breast was dry, but, who knew, maybe that was how the Amish liked it? The cookies looked suspiciously like standard wedding cookie table fare. The bottle of champagne, which suddenly didn't seem like that great a deal—there were six of us—wouldn't be delivered until just before midnight.

After dinner, the guys began to grumble about the after-party. Mary desperately tried to rally the troops and make sure this part of the night wasn't a total bust. Mary was no dummy. What do you do in an uncomfortable setting with a bar? You drink yourself comfortable, of course.

By eleven, we were all buzzed, boozy, or sloppy drunk. The girls were dancing without shoes, making friends with octogenarians on the dance floor, rocking out to "YMCA" and "Brown Eyed Girl." It was *Sweatin' to the Oldies* with a disco ball. The guys continued to sit and talk but seemed to be amused enough.

When the time came, we faked the words to "Auld Lang Syne" and made quick work of the bottle of C-grade Prosecco.

At the end of the night, no one was in any condition to drive. Ignominiously, we turned to Steve's dad, who graciously got out of bed to provide clown-car limo service to all six of us.

Back at my house, as her fellow celebrants secured glasses of water and padded surfaces on which to crash, Mary could not hide, through the redness in her eyes, a look of self-satisfaction. The night at the Bradley House may not have been the glamorous, debaucherous soiree Mary had imagined, but it had been memorable, and we had gotten very, very drunk.

"Well guys, that was fun," Mary slurred. "Wanna book next year?"

5. "Y'ALL, I THINK WE NEED MORE HAIRSPRAY"

"Meg," Mary said. "I'm *screwed.*"

The year was 2001 and we had just finished "hell week" for "Steel Magnolias" at the beautifully restored Grand Theater, now Mon River Arts, in Elizabeth, Pennsylvania. As sometimes happens, the production was cursed with bad luck. The week before opening, tech week, or "hell week," is when many final preparations for a show are made, and, significantly, when the cast members work through lines that won't stick. Many "Steel Magnolias" cast members missed all or part of the week with bad colds. Mary caught it last and missed the final run-through before the show opened.

"Mare," I said. "We got this. I can do a read through with you."

"A read through isn't gonna make the lines stick, Meg," Mary said. "That's what tech week was for!"

"What are you going to do, Mary?" I said. I cut myself off because I didn't want to give her an out.

Mary raised her eyebrows in a way I recognized immediately. Close friends have ways of communicating wordlessly, and Mary and I had a whole unspoken *language*. Mary had, in effect, flipped the question back to me: How was I going to help her?

Some backstory: When the audition call went out for "Steel Magnolias," I was excited. Though I had never seen Robert Harling's 1987 play performed, I was familiar with the 1989 film adaptation starring a virtual "who's who" of actresses of the era. Mary, though, was less than enthused. With her lights-out voice, Mary preferred musicals; straight plays, in her view, deprived her of the chance to put her best foot forward. Mary underrated her chops as an actor, but I knew how versatile she was. I also didn't want to do the show alone. I'd gone into full-on persuasion mode, playing up the movie and the powerful performances that made it so memorable.

When callbacks were finished, Mary was cast as Truvy Jones, the initially shy beauty-school graduate who moves to Chinquapin Parish in northwestern Louisiana. My role was Annelle Dupuy, whom Truvy hires to work in her home-based beauty parlor. Rounding out the cast were the amazing Miss Heather Marie on double duty as Shelby and the hilarious Laurie London Ouiser, and the lovely Diana Neil Michael as Clairee. Designers Ken, Rob, and Ernie put long hours into building an elaborate set that actually had running water so that Annelle could shampoo hair on stage.

Mary's problem was also mine because I'd talked her into auditioning for the play in the first place—but that wasn't the only reason. In a play, the cast is a single, connected unit: If one piece is shaky, the integrity of the whole show is compromised. It followed that, if Mary was "screwed," so was I, and so was the rest of the cast.

To say I was stressed would be an understatement: I needed to come up with a solution both to save Mary and keep the whole show from tanking. The next day or so, the problem became my "screensaver": Everywhere I went, everywhere I looked, visions of Mary flubbing her lines danced before my eyes. Then, as I was rinsing my hair, an idea washed over me. Because our characters worked in the beauty salon, Mary and I had "workstations." I could tape handwritten notes to each of our stations—this way, if either of us got lost, we could simply refer to the note and get back on track.

That night, I arrived early with my scraps of paper ready to go. When the rest of the cast was in makeup, I sneaked onto the stage and taped the notes in strategic places around the set.

When I showed her my handiwork, Mary didn't know whether to laugh or cry. But she was desperate. "You're a *genius*," she said.

"Let's see how it goes," I said.

The idea worked like a charm until the first Sunday matinee performance. In one scene when we were both at center stage—nowhere near the damn notes—Mary "went up" on a line (theater-speak for forgetting). Using our unspoken language, Mary gave me pleading eyes that said in no uncertain terms, "This was your stupid idea, Meg! Help me!"

The moment seemed to last forever. I didn't know what to do.

At last, Mary improvised. As though her character were making small talk, she said simply, "What do you think, Annelle?"

I sensed what Mary was trying to do and made it a ditzy bit: "Y'all, I think we need some hairspray!"

This gave me an opportunity to sprint offstage and refer to the script. I leaped back onto the stage and brought us to the next line. Mary knew the cue, nailed her line, and we were back on track. The rest of the night, we *killed.*

Friends in the audience later reported, perhaps out of kindness, that they didn't realize anything was amiss. Mary and I chose to believe them.

As a postscript: "Line-gate" wasn't the only mishap during the run. After a Saturday evening show, the actress playing M'Lynn came down with a sudden, debilitating affliction and could barely finish the show. Laurie Lowe Watson had to replace her for the next day's matinee and acquitted herself fabulously. At one point, it was storming outside and the power went out on stage. Finally, the stage lights came back on. My character, Annelle, had just undergone a religious awakening in the play, so I extemporized, "Praise the Lord! It's a miracle!" The audience, who were pulling for us, erupted into laughter.

One day, after a matinee, my dad was in the lobby being the "stage dad" he always was. When he saw Mary in her show wig, he hugged her and gave her a thumbs-up: "Love the new hair, Mare Mare."

Mary burst out laughing: "Thanks, Mr. May. It's a Captain Hook wig I bought at a party store!"

Still dressed in my Annelle costume, I laughed so hard I almost knocked off my fake, pregnant belly.

6. HERE COMES THE BRIDE . . . OR NOT

It was Mary and Ryan's wedding day at Mary's family's church, the Christian Center in Belle Vernon, Pennsylvania. The sanctuary was decorated. The ushers were ready. The guests had begun to arrive outside the church. There was only one problem: Mary was missing.

In true Mary style, the wedding was like a Hollywood event. Mary had chosen a pricey designer gown that they had to alter by half because she kept losing weight on the "wedding stress" diet. Kissy, Mary's beautiful stylist, did her hair in my favorite look for Mare: dark and long with spiral curls. Mary wore an actual crown atop her head.

Mary's wedding party was huge—nine or ten bridesmaids and groomsmen, a junior bridesmaid, and two flower girls. I was "matron" of honor and Mary's beautiful friend Amy was "maid." The guest list was enormous. Mary's dad was a minister at the church (as he always said, "Don Johnson, not from Miami Vice, but a soldier for Christ!"), so half the congregation had been invited, in addition to people from Mary's life past and present.

I wouldn't say Mary was a "bridezilla" exactly, but she definitely had a vision and wanted every piece—and there were many pieces, including a "dove release" after the ceremony—to fall into place for the big day. The presiding minister, Pastor John, was on the same page, and could not have been more emphatic that things needed to be "on time" and "on schedule."

A point of contention had been whether alcohol should be served at the reception. Mary was a preacher's daughter, and her immediate and extended family, in addition to most of her family's friends, were deeply religious. The prevailing feeling was that God and liquor did not mix, and that the reception should therefore be dry. Mary's fiancé, Ryan, was of a strongly differing opinion. In his view, he was paying for the reception, so the choice should be his and Mary's. The discussion between Mary and Ryan had gone on and on . . . and on.

"You think I don't want to get my drink on, too, Ryan?" Mary had said. "*Especially* after this conversation?"

At last, a compromise was reached: There would be no bar, but a champagne toast. The wedding would be "dry-adjacent."

We were assembled in the church, getting ourselves organized. This seemed to be taking a long time; we were all whispering and looking around, either for Mary to materialize or for someone to tell us what to do. A half-hour became an hour. Some guests had been seated and others were milling around the vestibule and the area in front of the church. I kept thinking, "Good thing Mary's dad is a minister here, or we'd be in trouble!" Then my thoughts turned to Mary. I knew she had been nervous; what if she was doing a "runaway bride" thing? There was no way for me to reach her and our beautiful friend Angela Marie, who had also gone missing.

Finally Mary appeared, looking radiant but visibly perturbed. I ran over to her. "Oh my GOD, Mary, I was worried sick!" I said. "What the hell happened?"

From behind her makeup, Mary let out a long, dramatic sigh. "There was a *huge* issue with the wedding programs, Meg. Somebody was about to get their ass whooped!"

Mare's attention to detail meant having no wedding programs or programs with tons of errors wasn't going to happen. She needed the issue fixed immediately—but several hundred programs could not be printed immediately. (I do need to say that not all of Mary's ideas were great. She had, after all, insisted on Ryan getting a perm for my wedding.)

Mary had just finished saying "whooped" when Pastor John and Mr. J. rounded the corner. From there, things moved quickly. The remaining guests were seated. Aided by muscle memory, the wedding party re-formed into a neat line for the opening procession. Reverend Johnson stood with Mary. Bach's unfortunately titled "Air on a G String" began. The line began to move. The nightmare was restored to a Disney dream.

I had never seen Mary and Ryan so happy. The reception was one of the best times Steve and I ever had. The good times were aided, in part, by the champagne, bottles of which were low-key flowing everywhere. We toasted the hell out of the happy couple.

When the night was over, I made my way over to Mary and whispered, "Another journey started."

"Meg, honey, we're on the *same* journey," Mary said.

And she was right.

7. A SHOWER-AND-A-HALF / "AWWW . . . SHE'S SMILING"

When I was pregnant with my daughter Michaela, I actually had one and one-half baby showers—thanks to Mary.

Steve's family, the Mitchells, did most of the planning for the first, at the Skyview Volunteer Fire Department in West Mifflin. My mother-in-law's brother-in-law, Terry, was the fire chief. The space was large, we had a family connection, and it was blocks away from our house.

Donna and Steve's sister Tammy knew and loved Mary, so of course she was involved in planning the shower, too, and Mary never did anything halfway. Still, though she didn't say anything, I had the sense that Mary was giving the whole celebration side-eye. Mary was not a "fire hall" kind of girl; though her resources were limited, she always wanted top-shelf everything for herself and her bestie.

Less than a month before my approaching due date, September 2, 2003, Mary told me matter-of-factly, "I'm throwing you a shower."

"But Mare," I said. "I already *had* a shower. No one needs *two* showers!"

"Meg, the shower you had was *nice*," Mary said, letting the last word linger. "But this is your first child! You are my best friend! We need to do it up *right*!"

"What if I'm in labor?" I said. "What if I've already had the baby?"

"Didn't your doctor say you were going to be late?" Mary said. "First babies are always late. And don't worry, we'll plan it out so that there's time on the back end just in case the baby does come early. I *got* this."

There was no sense in fighting it because when it came to decisions, Mary was like Ramses in *The Ten Commandments*: "So let it be written. So let it be done!"

The date was set for August 23. The invites went out. Mary had rented the community room in the Pleasant Hills Community Presbyterian Church, a more intimate space than the Skyview and the former home of the Christian Drama Workshop, where I had acted in several productions. In classic Mary style, she had every detail planned to perfection, from theme to decorations to a massive food spread. To be on the safe side, Mary went with a neutral color scheme. She knew the nursery was baby blue and yellow with baby zoo animals. I desperately wanted pink, but the sonographer had been consistently noncommittal about gender: "I *think* it's a girl, but maybe hold off on the pink."

The day before the shower, August 22, I'd had an OB/GYN appointment—the baby was still really far up, and there was zero dilation. This was what I had been told to expect, so I wasn't disappointed. With the shower coming up, I got a manicure. That evening, Steve and I went to Burlington Coat Factory to get decorations and outlet covers for the nursery. I noticed some mild cramping but thought little of it. On the way home, we stopped at Steve's favorite restaurant, Damon's: The Place for Ribs, in Pleasant Hills. I wasn't super hungry and settled on a Mexican-style appetizer—rumor had it, some spice could "rev up" the delivery process.

Back home, Steve and I were on the way to the nursery upstairs when my water broke. Steve actually thought I had peed my pants. We called my OB/GYN; they said I was in labor and was at risk for having a "dry birth," so we needed to get to Magee Women's Hospital in Oakland ASAP. Steve brought my sodden pants just in case it was all a false alarm. When we arrived, there was a *Halloween* movie marathon playing in the admittance room.[4] Mary certainly would have rushed to be there with us, were it not for the small matter of the shower, which she was busy putting the finishing touches on.

In theater, the show must go on—and so it was with my second baby shower. I think Mary held out hope that I would have the baby in thirty minutes, clean up, and bring her to the shower. Unfortunately, labor takes time, and I didn't have Michaela until the party was about to start.

The shower became a celebration. My friend Misty Wilds-Chillingworth was pregnant, too, at the time—we had just reconnected after a few years in the wilderness of post-graduate life. A fellow Point Park musical theater major, Misty

---

[4] For some people, this might have been a bad omen, but the *Halloween* franchise has always been a favorite of my sister Jenny's and mine. Coincidentally, a *Halloween* marathon was also on TV in the waiting room almost five years later when Steve and I arrived at the same hospital for my labor with Max.

had no problem standing in for me as the requisite pregnant person and opening the gifts in my stead. Of course, by then, there was no need for a neutral color scheme. Michaela May Mitchell[5] entered the world at 2:54 p.m.—just in time for the cake.

* * *

Mary was the first person to call me in the hospital and had visited me as soon as she could,

---

[5] We settled on "Michaela," if the baby was a girl, at the end of a long process. My Nanny's name was "Margaret" and I'd always loved the Rod Stewart song "Maggie May," but Steve was a hard "no" on that one. A second choice was "Paige Elizabeth," and Steve reluctantly assented, but I made the mistake of revealing my name choice to my colleague at the Art Institute whose due date was before mine. When her daughter was born in July, she revealed the name to be none other than . . . Paige Elizabeth. Back to the drawing board. For a long time, Steve and I could not agree. We thought, if our child was a girl, the name would be "Baby Girl Mitchell"—sort of like "The Artist Formerly Known as Prince." Finally, we came to "Michaela." I loved it because, to me, it sounded Irish. Also, my Nanny had loved a show called *Dr. Quinn, Medicine Woman*, in which Jane Seymour played "Michaela Quinn." To seal the deal, Steve had a cute female friend in college they called "Mike"; the idea was that "Michaela" would be shortened to "Mike," but instead she became "Lulu" and, later, "Kayla."

post-cleanup. After Steve and I brought Michaela home, Mary and Mrs. Johnson were the very first people to arrive at our house, armed with easily ten disposable cameras (this was before most people had digital cameras). Mary proceeded to take pictures of Michaela, me and Michaela, Steve and Michaela—*everyone* with Michaela—from every possible angle.

"Mary," I said. "I don't think you need that many pictures. She's just sleeping right now."

As Mary edged in for another shot, her posture changed. "Ooo! She's smiling at me!" she said. "Look at the corners of her mouth!" Mary's voice shifted into high-pitched baby talk: "Little Michaela's *smiling* at her Aunt *Mare*. Beautiful smiling *baby* Michaela!"

I looked closely but couldn't really see what Mary was talking about—as best I could tell, Michaela's mouth had opened to facilitate breathing. I had seen this "sleeping mouth" on Steve's face many times. Michaela was a gorgeous baby, but no smile was happening.

Mary insisted that I had missed the moment and could not be swayed: "I know what I saw, Meg. It was a smile!"

When the photoshoot was over, Mary rushed off to a one-hour development place—Mrs.

Johnson was hanging out with the crowd that had assembled at my house—then hurried back.

When the photos were unveiled, the whole room was in stitches: Mary had, for all intents and purposes, shot ten rolls of exactly the same photo—Michaela: pink and inert, beautiful and unsmiling. Though the angles and people around Michaela changed, it was as though the infant had been cut and pasted from one picture to the next.

Though Mary was forced to admit that she didn't "get" the smile in the photo, she was unbowed. "I still know what I saw!" she maintained. "She knew her Aunt *Mare who loves her so much* was looking at her."

A new, unbreakable bond had been forged.

8. IT'S A GIRL

Like sisters, Mary and I always followed each other in life; whatever stage one of us was in, the other was either right there or just behind. I loved this because it gave both of us a soulmate with whom to share these experiences. We graduated together and married within two years of each other. I desperately wanted Mary to join me on the motherhood journey. She had been trying for a while and, like many women, was struggling a bit, emotionally, with the wait and the uncertainty. She wanted it so badly.

Mary and I met for lunch as often as we could, usually in the food court at Oxford Centre, and things were pretty routine: We would both get salads and sit and chat about our days. Today, though, when Mary came down the escalator to meet me, she had a strange, almost twisted expression on her face.

Before she was even seated, opposite me, she was talking: "Meg, my period is really late, but I feel like it's definitely coming. It's making me nauseous."

"Oh my God," I said. "Mare, you are SO pregnant. You need to get a test now!"

Mary hurried to CVS to get a pregnancy test. To save time, I got our salads. The plan was for Mary to take the test in her company's bathroom, then come down the escalator with either a "thumbs-up" or a "thumbs-down." I waited as patiently as I could, just picking at my salad. After what seemed like most of our lunch break, Mary appeared on the escalator. I could see the sadness and disappointment in her eyes, and my fears were confirmed when I saw her thumb was pointed down. Then she started laughing and popped both thumbs way up. Pure joy.

I gave Mary the biggest hug imaginable. We were jumping up and down in the middle of the Oxford Centre food court as if we'd won a Chevrolet on *The Price Is Right*, oblivious to anyone else.

The pregnancy was not easy. Mary suffered from gestational diabetes and overall did not feel well for pretty much the whole ten months she was pregnant. At twenty weeks, Mary discovered she was having a baby girl. The child already had a name: Kennedy Grace. She would be born right before Christmas. I don't know who was more excited: Mary, Ryan, or me.

The day finally arrived. Mare's water broke on December 18, a few days before Christmas. I had Steve pick me up so that we could get Michaela from daycare and be there right before the delivery. We arrived. "Kay" was literally running all over the place with one tiny ponytail, with almost no hair on the top of her head to put in it. We waited and waited.

I couldn't understand what was taking so long because Mare's belly had really dropped. Kennedy was so low she could almost walk out of her mother's uterus. Like her mother, though, she was stubborn; not ready, she was fighting to move her head up into "breech" position. We were there for hours and hours, feeding Mary ice chips, chasing Michaela, hoping the moment would come. Finally, the decision to perform a C-section was made. The surgery was scheduled for a few hours later.

Michaela, who was up way, way, way past her bedtime, had started melting down. Steve and I accepted that there was no way we could stay and promised to return after the baby was born.

We were halfway home when my flip phone started ringing. It was Ryan: Kennedy Grace Blocher was born at 9:45 p.m., just after we gave up and left.

This was before the days of Facebook and Instagram. When everyone emailed pictures of the new baby, I was so jealous. With my own child and job—Kennedy was born on a Tuesday —I had to wait until I got off work and picked Michaela up at daycare before I could finally get to the hospital to meet the baby.

I fell immediately in love. We all did—especially Michaela, who wasn't even one and a half. It warms my heart so much that the girls remain close now.

It almost goes without saying that I, of course, took a day off on September 4, 2009, when Mary's son, Daunte Ethan, was born. I was literally the first person the doctor handed the baby to. I was not going to miss out again.

9. CALIFORNIA (KNOWS HOW TO PARTY)

It was spring 2004. Michaela was just over six months old, and Mare was visibly pregnant with Kennedy. My little sister Katie, who had waited for Michaela to be born before moving to California, was still freshly arrived in Santa Monica, living in her own place not far from her best friend Shannan, also known as "Pops," in Marina del Rey.

I couldn't wait to get out to visit Katie and see the glamorous life I imagined she was living. Mary was always down for a trip. As usual, neither of us had any money, but you only live once, so the decision was made to take the leap and head west for a long weekend.

When Katie picked us up at LAX, we were very much weary travelers, not to mention like deer in headlights—more like the sunlight of bright LA. Mary and I were awestruck by the sun, the palm trees, and by Katie herself, who looked stunning in her carefully selected outfit: slim-fit white jeans and a looser-fitting top, azure blue in a way that recalled the beautiful Pacific.

Mary and I were both hungry from the hours-long flight, so Katie zipped into a drive-thru. I told Katie we didn't need drinks—we still had the pop we'd bought at the airport in Pittsburgh—but she insisted. Katie tried to go "big" with everything she did, so we shouldn't have been surprised that she got what appeared to be the largest-possible-size drink to go along with our chicken tenders and fries.

As Katie was transferring the drinks to me, the lid on one of them popped off. As if in slow motion, I could see the cola rise in an "arc" trajectory, then fall with a cold splash onto my lap, drenching me. It was as I was swatting ice cubes off my legs that I noticed, with horror, a brown spot about the size of a Kennedy fifty-cent piece on Katie's electric white jeans.

"Oh great, Mo," Katie said. "You spilled pop on my new pants!"

I didn't know whether to laugh or cry. I chose option three: Keep a straight face and try to empathize. I knew I had to keep my focus on

Katie's perceived misfortune, not my own dousing.

"Those are beautiful jeans," I said. "I'm sorry that happened."

"*Were* beautiful jeans, Mo," Katie fumed.

I would have given anything to see the look on Mary's face.

That night, after a necessary costume change (I did some shirt wringing in the bathroom), we visited with Katie and "Pops" at Katie's place. Mary and I must have seemed so old to Katie and Shannan. Even though I was only twenty-nine, and Mary twenty-eight, the five-or-so-year age difference seemed massive. Whereas Mary and I were both married, Katie and Shannan were just getting started in the LA dating scene. Whereas Mary and I were both mothers, children weren't even a twinkle in Katie and Shannan's eyes—yet. As anyone who becomes a parent learns, the distance between the salad days of post-adolescence and adulthood isn't nearly as great as it can sometimes seem when you're young and free.

As the night wore on, Katie seemed eager to have a more confidential check-in with Shannan.

"You look tired, Mo," she said.

"But it's not that late," I said. And it was true: LA was three hours behind Pittsburgh.

Katie produced a pill. "Take this," she said. "You'll sleep great."

With some hesitation, I did as I was told.

Later, as I faded blissfully from consciousness, I saw all the pretty colors in a psychedelic rainbow of love, joy, and peace.

I was deeply impressed by the way my sister had adapted to life in sprawling LA. Katie had chutzpah in spades: On one shopping expedition, I watched in awe as Katie haggled with a shop assistant to get me a geisha-inspired sexy dress to wear for my upcoming thirtieth birthday. Katie seemed to know her way around (this was in the days before Google Maps and Waze), and her "fake it till you make it" approach definitely applied to life in the fast lane. I was a little bit terrified by the way my baby sister maneuvered through the treacherous intersections and freeways. Though Katie did a good job of manifesting "unfrazzled," I saw my life flash before my eyes at least twice on the way to The Comedy Store on the Sunset Strip. Mary and I laughed a bit harder than the comedy warranted, thrilled to still be alive.

The next day, Katie had a date that she was unable or unwilling to postpone. Mary and I were supportive—Katie had gone so far out of her way for us, and we could understand her desire to stay connected to her new life. Also, this would give Mary and me an opportunity to shop and grab lunch on our own. Katie insisted that we use her car and proceeded to give Mary what sounded like confusing-as-hell directions. Mary, typically a confident driver, was apprehensive: She didn't know the roads, was still scarred from the night before, and desperately wanted to keep, intact, the growing baby in her uterus.

Mary let out a muted version of her cackle. "Um Katie," she said. "Girl, that's a lot. We can just get dropped off and walk around. You can pick us up later."

Imagine a red coupe screeching over to the side of the road, the door swinging open, and two road-weary travelers teetering out on the highest of heels. This was Mary and I on Rodeo Drive. We spent the next several hours scouting for LA baby clothes, stylish yet affordable maternity wear, and a chew-safe toy for

Michaela. As Katie's date was going to be on the long side, Mary and I stretched the shopping out for as long as we could. At the time, Mary was in her "short wig" phase; though she must have been sweltering beneath the wig, she was a trooper and didn't complain once.

Finally, the need for sustenance began to overtake us. Far from home and short on cash, we were craving familiar junk food—burgers and fries would have been perfect—but every restaurant was health conscious or vegan, prohibitively expensive, or only sold green smoothies. We finally found a restaurant with outside seating that at least had chicken fingers. Mary and I, trying to economize, split an order and washed it back with cups of water.

By the time Katie's car skidded over at the predetermined corner, Mary and I were sweaty, exhausted, sore-footed, and starving. Katie, sensing our desperation, generously ordered a massive pizza. On the way home, she asked us many questions about our day, offering her commentary on each of our stops but was characteristically cagey with details about her date.

Later, as we were tearing into the food, Mary cut to the chase: "Okay, Katie, start giving us the scoop on the damn date!"

If I had said this, Katie would have shut me down and insulted me to boot. As an honorary May sister, however, Mary held some sway, and Katie haltingly shared some scattered information, from which we could glean that the date had been inconclusive.

Later, as we were lounging around Katie's place, Mary and I calculated how much time we'd need in the morning to get to the airport. As this was back in the era of flip phones, we decided we'd require an actual alarm to wake us at the proper time.

Mary took the lead: "Katie, can you set your alarm clock for our early flight tomorrow?"

"I don't have an alarm clock," Katie said matter-of-factly.

Mary couldn't resist an eyebrow raise. "How do you know when it's time to wake up?"

"Oh," Katie said. "I'm just really good at waking up at the right time." She paused, then offered, by way of explanation: "I have an alarm clock in my head."

Mary looked at me pleadingly for backup, but there wasn't anything I could do: Katie was the host, and if she claimed to have an alarm clock "in her head," we were going to have to go with it and hope for the best.

That night, tired from our adventures, we all slept well. Too well, it turned out: Mary and I woke up an hour late; Katie, meanwhile, was still fast asleep. As Mary and I rushed to get ready—we couldn't resist a few mutterings between us about Katie's internal alarm clock malfunctioning—Katie popped innocently into the bathroom to deliver one of her patented truth bombs: "Girls, I don't think you're gonna make it!"

As it turned out, we didn't make it. With a couple of lucky passengers comfortably ensconced in our seats, Mary and I found a quiet corner within view of the gate and waited calmly for the next flight.

Where possible, it's best to take what the world gives. We had wanted to get a taste of Katie's new life. If we wound up getting some bonus time to linger in its afterglow, who were we to complain?

10. BAKING WITH THE "BVM"

It was 2006. At the time, Mary and I both felt overextended with our jobs and roles as parents, but we were young. Life was simpler and easier than it would become. Theater was a constant for both of us, and a through line within that constant was the show *Nunsense*. By now, we were on our third production and third theater playing Sister Mary Amnesia and Sister Mary Hubert.

Mary and I had so much fun with these characters: They had become part of our bodies, and we could morph into these "sisters" at a moment's notice.

This particular performance was for South Park Theater in Allegheny County's South Park. This was the show where we first met fellow actor Mary Kay Randolph, and "The Three Ms" were born. It was also where we met the beautiful and talented Lorraine "Lo Lo" Corpora

Mszanski, who went on to direct many plays on the South Park stage and now runs the theater. The production also reconnected us with friends Kathy Hawk and Michelle Roper Rivas.

We rehearsed a *lot*. The director soon learned that, anytime the clock struck nine fifteen, Mary and I would become punch drunk and goofy, and nothing new would stick in our heads at all—forget blocking or choreography. Still, if anything, we were ready to go two weeks before our opening. This gave us the opportunity to play a bit and occasionally prank each other, getting each other to break character as the scenes and circumstances allowed.

In one of my favorite scenes in *Nunsense*, "Baking with the Blessed Virgin Mary (BVM)," the sisters are trying to sell quirky cookbooks to raise proceeds to bury several dead nuns they are storing in the convent freezer (following their untimely, accidental deaths due to tainted vichyssoise soup). This scene featured The Three Ms.

In the *Nunsense* script, the sisters appropriate a middle school stage set up for a production of "Grease." In our production, because the set wasn't important (the script just says we're borrowing the stage from our students), we used the dressed set from the previous production, a period piece involving all kinds of old, dusty, medieval books. When we needed a book to use as the huge "Baking with BVM" cookbook, we selected the biggest, oldest, dustiest volume we could find and slapped a cover on it. Done.

During one of the performances, this "cookbook" caused things to go hilariously off the rails. Mary was in the middle of reciting her lines—"This book is chock full of recipes perfect for the Catholic kitchen"—when she flipped to a page depicting a series of images of sex positions from the Kama sutra.

Even from my place on the stage, I could clearly see an array of clinical schematics of couples practicing impossibly bendy sexual poses. Obviously, we were not expecting this. The proverbial needle scratched off the record. I looked at Mary. Mary looked at me. We both looked at Mary Kay. As actors, we were trained to be in control of our composure, but the ridiculousness of the situation was just too much. I can't remember who broke character first, Mary Kay or me, but it was a struggle to recover.

Mary had somehow found a way to earmark the racy pages. For the rest of the show, she kept purposely turning to them right before Mary Kay or I had to talk. At one point, all of us were unabashedly laughing. It was all I could do to maintain composure of my bladder; our nun costumes were layers upon layers and it would have been hard to "go" fast.

At one point, the script called for my character to present a horrible makeshift book stand held together with two loose nails. On went the tome with the Kama sutra poses. I could barely hold it together. Fortunately, this was in keeping with my Mary Amnesia character, whose tagline is, "Nice House, Nobody Home." I never laughed as hard as I did when we finally got off the stage. With Mary and Mary Kay, The Three Ms, it was a proper laughing fit.

Our hysterics must have been audible outside of the theater, all the way into South Park's playgrounds and picnic pavilions, all the way up into Heaven above, with Mary's huge, contagious cackle leading the way.

For actors, theater is not only art and craft but a source of joy.

11. LIKE MOTHER, LIKE DAUGHTER

One afternoon, Mary and I were sitting with the girls at Ruby Tuesday at Century III Mall. Kennedy was three and Michaela was four and change. Kennedy, affectionately known as "Mush," was testing boundaries: getting up from her seat, fidgeting, banging silverware, trying to loop Michaela in—all normal behavior for a toddler.

Mary was telling a story about her job at Union Real Estate and, more than once, needed to stop what she was saying to redirect Kennedy. Each time, Mush would stop for a few seconds or maybe a minute; once Mary had started talking again, the impish grin would reappear on Kennedy's face and she would return to her "project."

The growing ire on Mary's face was unmistakable. Mary was the kind of person who was always in charge, yet here was this mini-me pushing her buttons to get her attention. As Mary and Kennedy were already in a kind of chaotic synchronicity, Kennedy knew exactly which buttons of Mary's to push, and vice versa. It became a matter of who would blink first.

There had never been any doubt that Mary and Kennedy would be close. Mary could not wait for Kennedy's arrival; I think she had her name picked out in college. Kennedy's middle name is Grace. There might have been a moment of moving Grace into the first-name slot, but, if so, it was fleeting—I don't remember Mary ever waffling on Kennedy.

Mary was pretty much a stereotypical Gemini: all in, all the time, loud and proud, loving, impulsive. Kennedy was a classic Sagittarius: curious, adventurous, and blunt. In astrology, Gemini and "Sagis" form a square aspect, which results when planets are ninety degrees apart. The energies can be volatile because their elements are connected: Fire needs air to burn. But the fact that both signs are grouped under the same mutable aspect can also cause friction.

As with their signs, Mary and Kennedy were always engaged in a kind of dance with each other: both smart and strong as hell, hard-working, stylish, stubborn, always late, and not about the fucking bullshit. In a fight between the two, nobody was backing down.

Kennedy was Mary's "mini" in many ways—even in her tiny stature. The marked difference was that, although she tried to keep it under wraps, Kennedy, like me and her father Ryan, was sensitive and easily stung.

With daughters just over a year apart, Mary and I were so excited to do "girl" days. Malls were our favorite. The path would always be the same: the Children's Place, Claire's Boutique, some junky place with toys, the bookstore, the pet store if there was one, a carousel or some other spinning thing to make the girls queasy, and finally lunch at a restaurant you could enter from inside or out. This meant either South Hills Village, Red Rocket, or—at Century III—Ruby Tuesday (I loved the salad bar). Michaela and Kennedy, Virgo and "Sagi," were literally a match made in heaven, linked through the planet Venus. Together, we were an unstoppable foursome.

Back at Ruby Tuesday, three-year-old Kennedy was hiding under the table. Finally,

Mary snapped, her voice raised and sharp: "KENNEDY!!! KNOCK IT OFF!!!"

I saw Kennedy poke her head up from under the table—this time, as if to say, "Nope, I'm done." She put her adorable, tiny hands with painted nails up over her beautiful brown eyes. She was feeling emotional and didn't want anyone to "see" her. To give mother and daughter a breather, I scooped up my honorary niece and took her for a walk around the room. Before long, all was well, and we were chasing the girls down to Dairy Queen, but this episode was telling.

In future years, when Mary and Kennedy were at odds, my role was always to be "good cop": the person to offer shelter or escape. Once, I even came to scoop Kennedy up to my house for a whole weekend. Every time, I would hear Mary say some version of "Meg, that Kennedy and her mouth . . . . I'm not the one!"

In fact, Mary *was* the one for Kennedy—something apparent to anyone lucky enough to experience the two of them in action. "Mother and daughter" is a complicated proposition. I recognize this in my years of experience with my mom, whom I love dearly, and in my own special relationship with Michaela.

Mare and Kennedy had an incredible bond. The text messages and voicemails between the two showed a softer side to Mary that some didn't get to see. Mary never missed an opportunity to let her little "Mush" know how proud she was of her, how brilliant and beautiful she was and, above all, how much she loved her and always had her back.

When parents and children argue, it doesn't mean they aren't close. It sometimes means they are maybe a little *too* close—not just peas in a pod but different versions of the same pea.

Though I can never be Mary, I'm part of a small group of people who truly knew her in all her beautiful complexity. Mary may have loved hard, but she was soft and gooey inside.

In my relationship with Kennedy, I try to channel both of these sides, even as I maintain the role I've had since "Mush" was born. I'm strong enough to push back when necessary, but I will never stop showering my "niece" with the love and affection she deserves. For as long as I live, I will be there to "scoop" Kennedy up whenever and wherever she needs me.

12. THE BIRTHDAY BRAWL

It was my birthday weekend. The plan was to have a triple date with Mary and my big sister Jenny, along with our husbands, Ryan, Rich, and Steve. My mother-in-law Donna ("Meemaw") volunteered to babysit Michaela and toddler Max. Though Mary was very pregnant with Daunte, she was not the kind of person to let a good get together pass her by.

We began at P. F. Chang's at the Waterfront. The dinner was amazing: lots of laughter and stories as usual. From there, we headed over to the AMC-Loews to see *The Orphan*, a horror film about an international adoption gone wrong.[6] We grabbed our snacks and popcorn and settled in to watch. The cozy section with the comfy tilt-

[6] I've enjoyed horror films going back to John Carpenter's *Halloween* and the supremely creepy TV adaptation of Ann Rule's *The Deliberate Stranger* (not technically horror, but "horror-adjacent").

back chairs wasn't available, despite Steve's best efforts, so we were in the regular seating area. Mary was full-on pregnant and clearly uncomfortable, but she endured without complaint.

There are many ways to enjoy a movie and I am totally okay with some people getting more animated than others. What it comes down to is being aware of the people around you and not letting your enjoyment negatively affect the experience of those around you. Simply put, no one wants to be "that person," and no one wants to be the person seated anywhere near "that person."

Anyway, the previews began, and it became immediately obvious that the people in the seats behind us were all, to a person, "that person." We scanned the theater for another group of six seats: nada. Finally, we accepted that our experience might be sub-optimal and settled in.

For a while, the movie seemed to have a lulling effect on the group—similar to what happens when you hypnotize a room full of fighting toddlers with *Toy Story 2*—or maybe it was the sedative quality of whatever booze the people had quaffed prior to entering the theater finally kicking in.

About halfway through the movie—around the time the orphan, Esther, revealed to be a twenty-something psychopath named Leena, stabs her adoptive father to death with a kitchen knife—the people behind us roused. Once again, they began cursing, commenting loudly on the action on the screen, and predicting—mostly accurately, to their credit—what was going to happen next.

We were all annoyed, but Mary, who had been a trooper the whole night, was fuming. Finally, she stage-whispered: "Meg, maybe it's the hormones, but I'm gonna *snap*!"

Ryan decided to take one for chivalry. He turned around and, in a firm voice just a click above a whisper, said to the people, "Hey, we're just trying to watch the movie. Could you please keep it down?"

That should have been the end, but it wasn't. Then someone behind us let out a barrage of profanity at Ryan, and another person ill-advisedly deployed the term "White boy."

Mary had reached her limit. Though Mary could not have been prouder to be Black, the people she cared for comprised every possible skin color and background. For a best friend, she had chosen me: a person with practically no melatonin to speak of. Ryan, Mary's husband, was White, and their daughter and soon-to-be son were mixed. For Mary, any race-based insult, regardless of its source or target, had the equivalent effect of grabbing the electrified third rail of the New York City subway with both hands.

"OH HELL NO," Mary loud-whispered. She turned to face the offending group. "Don't you talk to my husband like that! He is right: We've been listening to your nonsense all night. You need to SHUT THE FUCK UP!"

Having already played the race card, the group now deployed the gender card: "Hey man, you better control your wife!"

Mary stood up. This was the only time I ever saw a pregnant woman take off her earrings like she was ready to throw down. And Mary wore clip-ons.

Everyone in our group tried to de-escalate and apply the brakes, but the damn train was already barreling past subway platforms. I saw my birthday unraveling.

Hoping to quash the fight, Ryan whispered, "She's PREGNANT."

The lone girl in the group behind us replied with, "She's not pregnant in her FACE. I can still punch her!"

We were accelerating perilously close to impact. I tried to act as a human shield to protect Mary from any kind of cross-row swing. Steve and Rich shepherded us up and out of the row, into the aisle, and toward the exit in the back of the theater. We caught the movie's end in the warm, red glow of the "Exit" signs.

Rich, a proud product of the mean streets of Delaware County, northwest of Philadelphia, slipped out and tracked down management.

Once in safety, we were given so many free passes that our next thirty triple dates would be paid for. Unlike Esther/Leena and John, we all made it out unharmed, if not unshaken.

Though I was not above going on the attack in verbal altercations among friends and family, I wouldn't have dreamed of saying anything to a group of people in a movie theater, no matter how obnoxious—even on my birthday.

Part of what makes best friends "best" is the superpowers they often seem to have. Even when she was pregnant, Mary was a fighter.

13. HEARTBREAK AND ROAD RAGE

I got the call as Steve was dropping me off for work at the Art Institute of Pittsburgh. There was a brightly painted T. rex statue in front of the entrance that had appeared a few years before as part of the Carnegie Museum of Pittsburgh's "DinoMite Days" public art event; we were approaching the statue when I picked up the phone. It was Mary.

"Meg, my mom died, oh my God, oh my God, they asked me if I wanted to go inside and see her before they take her!"

As I listened, I could feel my heart breaking. Mrs. Johnson was like a second mom to me; she never called me anything other than "May May." I had just sat with her in my parents' sunroom for my sister Jenny's baby shower. She had loved all the windows and the sun decorations my parents had hung on the walls (in case anyone lost track of what room they were in). She had looked great—dressed in church clothes, as usual, with hair and nails on point, as usual. And she had seemed as spry as ever: as quick-witted and classy as Mary, but wise and dignified in a way befitting a woman in her early seventies.

"Oh my God, Mare," was all I could say. "Oh my God."

"My mom, Meg. My fucking mom! I'm done. I'm fine. No, I'm done. What will I tell Kennedy?!"

"We're on our way!" I said.

Steve had known Mrs. Johnson for more than ten years. He was linked to her through me, through Mary, and through his best friend, Ryan. With steely resolve, he maneuvered the car through the morning's Downtown traffic and headed back to the suburbs from which we had all come.

The rest of the day was a blur of Pittsburgh gray and tears. It meant so much to me to be present for my best friend and attend to her every need. This is what friends do: When two friends become each other's *people*, neither of them is ever truly alone.

As evening began to descend, Mary settled, as people often do when their world has been shattered, on a trivial detail. Mary had fixated on the idea of going to work the next day. I recognized instantly that this was a terrible idea. Mary's emotions were, understandably, all over the place. One minute she would be sobbing; the next she would be telling a funny story about Mrs. Johnson and cackling with laughter; the next she would be sobbing again. How the hell was she going to get through a whole day of work as a property manager?

Mary's course, once set, was about as flexible as the Elizabeth Bridge. Still, it was my duty as her best friend to try to get her to see reason.

"Mare," I said. "Honey. This is ridiculous. Look at you!" I gestured at the pile of Kleenex distributed around the both of us. "This is literally why they have bereavement!"

"I need to go, Meg!" Mary sniffed. "It's my job!"

"You're just looking for normalcy," I said. "You're just trying to control the one thing you can control!"

"Thanks, Dr. Meg!" Mary said. "Really, though. There are things I need to do before people start arriving. Can you imagine how many people will be coming to town? I'm gonna need, like, a week off. Minimum."

I felt like I had to do something, but I had no idea what. And then, there it was: "Can I go with you?"

Mary's tone shifted to bemusement. "To my job?! Hell no."

"No," I said. "Can I ride with you to work? That way we can talk on the way there and back."

"Oh," Mary said. "That is actually a good idea, Meg."

Thanks, Mare, I thought to myself.

It was agreed.

The ride to work was sad. Though we were trying to hold it together, we both cried much of the way. Because I worked different hours than Mary, I arranged to leave the office early to accompany her on the ride home. My coworkers knew Mare and it wasn't a problem. Unfortunately, we ran into trouble before we even got onto the road.

Mary had a parking pass for the lot across the street from her office. Occasionally, the pass would fail to trigger the gate to let people out of the lot. It was extremely frustrating—all the more so when an attendant was absent from their post in the little parking lot house, leaving no one to help. Understandably, it really pissed Mary off.

This day was particularly bad: There was a line of cars behind us, and, despite Mary's repeated attempts, the "metal arm of death" would not budge. As Mary wrestled with her pass, holding it up to the sensor at different angles to no effect, cursing under her breath, the woman in the car behind us started laying on her horn.

I looked back as if to say, "Cool it," but this had no effect.

Now the woman behind us actually began bellowing out her car window: "WHAT'S WRONG WITH YOU? MOVE!"

In person, Mary could be sweet and generous, but, behind the wheel, even on her best days, all bets were off. Mary was a great driver, and she had zero patience for others who were not—a category into which I squarely fit. She also fell prey to, I hate to say, a sort of road-borne hypocrisy: Mary always wanted other cars to let her over into their lane, but she would get into an accident before she would let anyone pull in front of her. And good luck to anyone foolish enough to cut her off or say anything derisive to Driver Mare.

"Road rage," Mary once declared as she pursued a driver who had wronged her down a side street in the South Side. "It's a thing!"

Back in the parking garage, the day after Mary's mom died, with the woman screaming and her horn blaring, I could see the adrenaline flooding Mare's face with red.

I tried to reel her in: "Mare Mare, just leave it alone; it's been a hell of a day for you. It's not worth it!"

Mary's brown eyes, though, had hardened into a "glare of doom." All the pain and loss, the sense of abandonment and at-sea-ness one feels at the unexpected loss of a loved one, had transmogrified into a thrumming, throbbing, palpable hate for the woman in the car behind us. There would be no pulling my friend back.

Mary rolled down her window, and lifted her little body, "Dukes of Hazzard"–style, halfway out: "MY FUCKING PASS IS NOT WORKING, YOU DUMBASS BITCH! WOULD YOU LIKE ME TO DRIVE STRAIGHT THROUGH A FUCKING METAL ARM SO YOU CAN BE HOME FOR YOUR CHICKEN DINNER?" Then a pause. "LOOK FOR THE ATTENDANT, JERK!"

At this, the driver's side door of the car behind us swung open. The woman, thirtysomething with a classic "Karen" haircut—upside-down bob with a side part, bangs sideswept and cut at an aggressive, "power" angle—clip-clopped toward us, still in her work heels. Things were about to get ugly.

I yanked Mary back into the car and closed her window. The woman raised her arm as if to start banging; I motioned for her to come around to my side. She did. I rolled down my window.

"Um," I said, trying to project calm. "You never really know what's happening with someone, what they are facing. My friend Mary just lost her mother yesterday."

"Oh my God," the woman said, suddenly chastened. "I'm so sorry for your loss."

"My friend is in a lot of pain, and now we are trapped in this lot. I'm going to try to page the attendant," I said. Then to Mary, a whisper: "Mare, where is the number?"

As Mary scanned the side of the gate house, the woman apologized: "I had a terrible day at work and just wanted to get home. Your troubles are much greater. I'm so sorry."

I struggled to find a way to get someone on the phone. Meanwhile, Mary and the woman fell into conversation. By the time the attendant returned from wherever the hell he'd been, Mary and her fellow, would-be combatant were actually joking with each other. It was like something out of *Highway to Heaven*, with me in place of Michael Landon.

At long last, the metal arm rose. Mary steered the car out of the lot, then immediately pulled over to the side of the road and collapsed onto my shoulder in tears.

As I held her, Mary let go of the whole day of trying to hold her pain and grief inside. We sat there for a long time in the early autumn darkness. Mary took some deep breaths, regrouped, and, when she was ready, pulled her car back onto the road.

The rest of the ride was silent. Mrs. Johnson was gone, and no tears or jokes or episodes of road rage would bring her back, but we had each other. It was a terrible, beautiful moment in our friendship.

Finally, as Mary pulled up to my house, she looked at me. Her eyes were still stricken. "Meg, thanks for your help," she said. Now a grin appeared on her face. "You probably could have let it play out a little more, though. I'm pretty sure I could have taken her."

14. TRUE FRIENDS NAP TOGETHER IN PUBLIC

It was a fall Friday and Mary and I had no set plans. Word had filtered through that a local high school was performing *Sweeney Todd*. From the time I met her, Mary had always been a Stephen Sondheim devotee, and *Sweeney Todd*, with its dark, edgy script, had always been one of her favorite shows. We both thought it was strange for a high school theater program to be presenting a musical out of season, but that didn't seem to be an important detail. It was Sondheim: we'd have a chance to show up and support young performers, and the tickets would be dirt cheap. Done.

For once, we arrived early, snacks stowed in our purses. There was the usual preshow buzz in the air. The crowd was small for a musical, but this was understandable—it was the fall. Mary and I spent the time before the show catching up and leafing through the program for names we recognized.

Finally, the lights went down and the curtain rose. Out strode Anthony Hope and the "Demon Barber of Fleet Street." They began talking in fake British accents mixed with Pittsburghese. This was strange, I thought; what about the prelude? Not only was there no singing, there was no music at all. My eyes scanned the stage for an orchestra pit. Maybe, I thought, there was a smaller band off to the side somewhere. Nothing. Sondheim's musicals were truly "light operas" with practically no spoken dialogue. Granted, this was a high school production, but what the heck? Mary gave me a glance that said as much.

Frantically, I referred back to my program for an explanation, and there it was: "Original 1970 theatrical version by Christopher Bond." This was not the Sondheim version but a straight play. I gestured to Mary; we both made wide, "oh shit" eyes.

Mary and I were both mothers of small children. We were both coming off long weeks at work. We were tired even walking in, and all the talking without the respite of song had a hypnagogic effect on me. I found myself shifting in my undersized, high school theater seat, in search of the most comfortable and supportive position. My face went flush and my eyelids were as heavy as, well, a play about sexual violence, murder, and betrayal without the succor of song.

Poof. The next thing I knew, the actors were taking their final bows, the curtains were going down, and the house lights were coming up. I had literally slept through all but perhaps the first two scenes of the play. I felt embarrassed and mortified and guilty—as an actor, I knew well how much work, how much care, how much heart had gone into the performance, and I had shown the ultimate disrespect: I had gone to sleep.

It was then that I heard a loud, guttural snort on my left. My shoulder on that side was vibrating ever so slightly. I looked over and Mary was out cold, her head on my shoulder. I jostled a bit to wake her.

"Meg," Mary said groggily. She rubbed her eyes. "Is this intermission?"

"No, Mare," I said. "The show is over."

"What?"

"The play is over. See, everyone is leaving!"

Mary scanned the room. High school kids, parents, and grandparents that had not quite filled the place were collecting their things and heading up the aisle to the doors.

"OH MY GOD," Mary said. Another eye rub. "Well, how was it?"

I sighed. "Well, Mare, I couldn't tell you because I was asleep, too. We both slept through the whole damn thing."

By now, much of the crowd had filtered out. We tried to blend in with the stragglers in the hope that we wouldn't be noticed. There was a chance that the darkness had concealed us, but it was unlikely: Mary, after all, had those Broadway snores.

When the car doors were safely shut, Mary unleashed her laugh. I started laughing, too, and before long, we were both in tears about our impromptu nap.

As we were both feeling rested and refreshed, we headed to Applebee's for martinis and cheese sticks. Our evening would have a second act.

15. THE WINE GROUPON

Mary had gotten it into her mind that we'd take a trip to New York. She needed a break and had discovered a few new, "innovative" ways to do the trip on a budget.

"One word," Mary said. "Megabus."

"What?" I said.

"Megabus," Mary repeated. "Greyhound is over. You can get a Megabus to New York pretty much for free and the bus is way nicer—double-decker, with no crackheads in the station."

I had to admit that it sounded nice.

As we later learned, the reason there were no crackheads in the station was that there *was* no station: Ticket holders had to stand out in the Pittsburgh cold and wait for a bus to materialize. And, though Megabus trips were advertised for "as low as $1," plus a reservation fee, we wound up paying more, though the tickets were still pretty cheap.

The ride to New York was awful. We arrived late (of course) and had to sit in different aisle seats in the back of the second level. In advance of the trip, Mare had taken me to her hairdresser, Kissy, to get hair extensions. Strips of my fine, thin hair were braided tight, flat against my head, and the synthetic hair was literally weaved in. The first few days, this felt like the "hair" equivalent to wearing braces—tight and uncomfortable, particularly in the seat of a double-decker bus bouncing along the Pennsylvania Turnpike.

For her part, Mary was getting "bus sick" and walked past me a dozen times en route to the stairs and the bathroom below. Each time, she made a point of mentioning how hungry she was. We had both skipped breakfast and couldn't eat "real" food with the motion of the hell bus. I filled up on Swedish fish and Starbursts.

The mega nightmare finally came to an end. We checked into our hotel (no price hack there), whose dated lobby reminded me of Stanley Kubrick's "The Shining"; we half expected to see creepy twins covered in blood at the end of the geometric carpet in the long-ass corridors. Mary once again mentioned that she was hungry. I suggested we get some food, but Mary shut me down.

"That's what the Groupon is for," she said.

I sighed.

This was around the time when Mary was obsessed with Groupons, group-based discounts on activities offered via a website. The "group" piece was key: Enough people had to sign up for a "Groupon" for the discount to work. You could convince Mary to go anywhere and do anything—go to the opera, take a duck boat tour of Pittsburgh—if you simply had a Groupon. Mary had found a Groupon for a wine tasting class in NYC she said was a "steal." Pizza and snacks were included with the fee.

By the time we arrived at the wine class, our printed-out Groupons in hand, we were hungry as hell. We quickly realized that this was not just a random, fun thing—no, this was an actual wine tasting class. The teacher was asking questions rapid-fire, everyone had to participate, and, between cold calling on people, she was enlightening us with more information about wine than a layperson could possibly want. The other "students" in the room were not regular people, however: They were enthusiasts, connoisseurs, quaffing the teacher's wine knowledge like the aficionados of fermented grape juice they were.

Finally, the wine itself came out. Mary and I were adamant, at first, that we were strictly white wine drinkers; red was simply too bitter and not our speed. This caused some muttering among our fellow classmates, but we were not out to impress. The goal was to drink, eat, and be merry and, after a few tastes, we were well on our way—except when it came to eating.

Each time the teacher left the room, Mary and I would gaze hopefully at the door, trying to will the teacher to bring back something, anything for us to eat. Each time, she would return armed with yet another bottle of wine.

"I think she's fucking with us, Meg," Mary said.

"Are you sure the Groupon said there would be food?" I said.

"*Yes,*" Mary said hangrily. From her purse, she pulled the crumpled-up sheet of paper. "See: *Pizza and snacks.*"

"Maybe they ran out," I said.

"They better not have run out," Mary said. "I'm about to go *ham.*"

Only after the final round of tasting did the teacher ask whether we were "ready" for food.

"Hell, yes, I'm ready," Mary whispered to me.

Personally, with nothing to speak of in my stomach to absorb the alcohol, I was half-drunk and ready to eat my fucking arm.

With great ceremony, the food was brought out. The "pizza" was neither New York brick-oven fare nor Dominos; I'm not even sure it qualified as pizza. Arrayed before us was a surprisingly meager amount of crackers, each one with a dot of cheese and a dollop of tomato sauce. The "snacks" comprised further crackers and healthy, unsatisfying, and unfulfilling crap.

"Oh Jesus," Mary said. Then, her tone shifted, "Well, thank you Lord!"

I don't think it could be said that we dug in, but we ate as much as we could without drawing attention to ourselves. The other "students" must have been hungry, too, because the food was gone before the teacher finished telling us about the origins of each kind of cracker.

Mary and I were still starving and teetering on the edge of being properly drunk. We didn't teeter for long: When the white wine was gone, we laid into the red, tossing back, rapid-fire, mini-glasses of the stuff we said we couldn't stand.

In the process, Mary and I made friends with the entire room. It didn't matter that we were the only non–New Yorkers. We didn't care what people thought of us and, through being ourselves, we made everyone laugh. We invited all the other students back to our hotel for an after-party.

The rest of the evening was classic New York: a cab ride home and stale hot dogs from a street vendor. We finally passed out from hunger pangs, throbbing wine headaches, and exhaustion. The after-party would have to follow another Groupon, another night.

16. A TALE OF FOUR TITTIES

We had come to San Jose for my dear friend Nique Eagen's wedding. We were standing outside a lingerie boutique. Mary was insisting we go inside, but I was hesitant.

"Bras, Mare? Really?"

"Meg, you're the maid of honor! If you wear the raggedy strapless bra you brought, it could 'bust' open!"

I sighed.

"Seriously, I wouldn't trust that thing. Let's each get a hot-looking new bra. My treat!"

Though Mary and I were both in a more or less perpetual state of being broke, our pay cycles ran on different schedules. This "happy accident" saved us many of the times we ventured outside of our home turf in Pittsburgh: When one person was down to double or single digits in a bank account, the other person would cover, and vice versa.

This whole trip had been another one of our shoestring budget operations, but we didn't let that hold us back. Our adorable hotel—low-slung like a bungalow, surrounded by palm trees—reminded Mary and me of "Melrose Place." The surrounding neighborhood felt cozy and walkable, and we spent the bonus time we had walking around, exploring the area.

There were quirky boutiques everywhere, and shop owners had water, food, and treats for the little dogs that everyone seemed to have. Mary discovered a really cute cupcake shop. Though she was diabetic, Mary made an exception for the trip ("What happens in San Jose stays in San Jose"). She committed the hours to memory and fit in a stop every day we were there.

It was on one of our walks that we found the lingerie shop. Inside, I spent some time browsing noncommittally before Mary suggested we get measured.

When I was younger, I imagined that cup size was a fixed thing, like shoe size. As a teen and all through college, I was a B and, at times, an A, depending on the bra and how much dancing I was being made to do at Point Park. Various boyfriends commented on my flat chest, and I sometimes thought, in a passive, daydreamy way, about getting implants. My pregnancy with my second child, Max, took care of any "needs" I might have had in that area. (Menopause would, suffice it to say, seal the deal.)

"Mare," I said. "I'm a 34C. I'm good."

"When was the last time you were measured?" Mary said.

I had been measured for the bridesmaid dress, but that hadn't included cup size. The fact was that I wasn't sure I had ever been "officially" measured for a bra.

"I don't know, Mare," I said.

"We're doing it!" Mary said. "Let's go."

I had been expecting something in the C or maybe D range. Boutiques run small, of course, but, when our sizes came back, they were crazy. I was measured an F, and Mary, who was always busty, came back a G.

"G as in 'golf'?" Mary said.

The shop assistant nodded.

"Oh, sweet Jesus, a G," Mary said. "I could smother someone!" She cackled—as she did each time she told the story the next couple of days.

I had known Nique since morning kindergarten at Gill Hall Elementary School, where I had rescued her chocolate milk from a bullying kid. Nique has always been beautiful inside and out, and she had a wedding (and a truly wonderful husband, Tony) to match.

Mary and I were tempted to wear our fancy new bras on top of our clothing, but we didn't want to steal the show.

17. THE MAGIQUEST

Michaela was going to celebrate her birthday while we were on vacation—the first ever joint Mitchell/Blocher trip to Myrtle Beach, South Carolina. Ever smart and tech savvy, Michaela did her research and asked to go to a place called MagiQuest at the Broadway at the Beach entertainment complex.

The idea, as Michaela explained to us as we sat around the living room at our condo, was that we were supposed to purchase a magic wand and become a "Magi." Armed with the wand and a clue book, we would search for clues through several themed rooms, interacting on the way with a number of characters and mystical creatures.

"So basically it's a real-life video game?" Mary said.

"Yeah," Michaela said.

"Let's do this," Steve said, pumping his fists. "I love video games."

To me, it sounded like a "Scooby Doo" role-playing game cut with elements of "Harry Potter" to keep things contemporary.

I didn't want to be a wet blanket, but I had real concerns about my son, Max. Though he was only four, I had already started to notice differences in the way Max processed and interacted with the world around him. He had a number of fears that, if triggered, would set him off: clowns, ventriloquist dummies, and animatronic people and animals were just a few. It wasn't that Max's fears were irrational—if anything, it made total sense to be afraid of these legitimately creepy things—it was just that Max felt everything *more*. Even something moderately creepy would push him beyond his threshold and into legit terror. I was fairly certain that there would be a number of creepy things at MagiQuest.

The weather at the beach in August can be a bit touch and go. It was a little overcast as we departed in our two cars; then, boom, the sky opened up and we found ourselves in the middle of a blinding rainstorm. None of us had brought umbrellas, but the torrent was such that, in this case, they would have been of little use. Ever creative, Mary found a plastic shopping bag in her car and wrapped it around her perfect braids (her summer look).

Together, the two families made a run for it. When we got to "dry land," I was literally wringing out my hair and searching for a ponytail holder. My makeup was smeared, Marilyn Manson-style, and my clothes were all soaked through. I looked like a contestant in a Halloween-themed wet T-shirt contest.

Mary was trying to keep us upbeat: "Damn, Meg, going for the wet look?" Then to Steve and Ryan: "I hope the rain 'whetted' your appetite for fun!" Then the cackle—always the cackle.

I held it together, for which I was low-key proud of myself. We paid for admission and bought a battery-powered magic wand for each of the kids except poor little Daunte, who received one without "magic" because Mary thought that he wouldn't know the difference.

Clutching our "Eternal Books of Wisdom," we made our way into the "Stone Circle." At this point, I was grabbing handfuls of my clothes in an effort to wring them out incrementally. As we were making our way toward the "training" area, the ad hoc members of the "Max management" team—Mary, Michaela, and I—spied an animatronic knight on one side of our path.

"Uh, mom," Michaela whispered.

Mary smiled nervously and tried to edge between Max and the knight, but eagle-eyed Max had already locked in. After a few seconds frozen in place, having a "zoinks!" moment, Max began literally freaking out—his legs churning ineffectually in a "Scooby Doo" blur: "NOOOOOOO!"

With some effort, I scooped up my four-year-old, his arms and legs flailing, his nails digging into my arm, and sprinted past the knight, my shoes squishing as I went.

To his credit, Max recovered quickly—he was taken with his wand and eager to use it.

As Gen-Xers, the grown-ups all knew from countless episodes of *Scooby Doo* what to "doo" and split up. As usual, Steve and Ryan took the easy duty: actually playing the game with Michaela and Kennedy and their pink and red glowing swords. Mary and I, on Daunte and Max patrol, tried to scope out each room before entering to little avail. Max kept screaming and sprinting past anything he was leery of. Daunte, meanwhile, kept wondering why his "broken" sword was not lighting up.

"I don't know, Daunte," Mary kept saying, glancing at me to keep from laughing. "Keep trying!"

As we passed warily into the "Thunder Cave," Mary whispered to me, "Meg, you know what this 'quest' is missing? Alcohol."

We both lost it—until Max encountered the "Man in the Mist" and lost it himself, again.

In the end, the girls and their dads had a blast, Michaela had the birthday experience she had hoped for, and the rest of us survived. Who could say what adventures awaited?

18. ON THE WATERFRONT: OH JESUS, CUT IT OFF / WE WANNA BE SURPRISED

Mary and I had our regular spots, and one of them was the Waterfront, the sprawling, open-air shopping district built in 1999 on the former site of US Steel's Homestead Steel Works. Whatever the plan was—shopping with our daughters, or dinner and drinks out with the girls—there was a good chance we'd wind up at the Waterfront, in the shadow of the towering brick smokestacks, which, deprived of their smoke-spewing purpose, stood proudly but sadly, reduced to ornament.

Life wasn't exactly easy—we were both still mothers of small children and money had never stopped being tight. Still, though we were nearing the end of our thirties, this part of our life seems, looking back, young and innocent. The really hard times were yet to come.

It was a perfect spring day. With daughters Michaela and Kennedy in tow, Mary and I had spent the day shopping. As usual, Mary looked great. She was wearing a pastel, pink, empire-waisted, frilly top, her hair styled to perfection—she was in her pixie-ish, Halle Berry wig phase. We had made stops at Claire's and The Children's Place and were now at Justice, watching the girls trot toward the dressing rooms to try on armfuls of bathing suits for our upcoming beach trip.

Mary was so charismatic that people constantly approached her. It was as though they wanted to bask for a moment or two in her glow in the hope that some of it might wear off on them.

There we were, waiting for our daughters to begin the bathing suit fashion show, when a woman came bounding up to Mary, two little boys trailing behind her. The woman stopped and lightly touched Mary's shoulder. "You are SO beautiful in that color pink," the woman said.

"Thank you," Mary said, clearly touched, and smiled in her bright, infectious way.

Assuming a chatty, one-of-the-girls tone, the woman went on: "Do you know what you're having this time?" She gestured to Mary's belly region, obscured by the empire waist and frills.

Mary didn't blink; if anything, she smiled even more brightly than before. "Actually," she said, "Me and Ryan aren't finding out the gender this time. We wanna be surprised."

If the woman had been paying any attention to me, she would have noticed my look of abject horror. But Mary was an actor to the core: Once she had the spotlight, she was not about to give it up—even when things had gone off the rails.

The two continued to chitchat about the "pregnancy." The woman floated several possible name suggestions for both genders. They were laughing and telling birth stories like two old chums. When Kennedy emerged from the dressing room in a bathing suit, the woman made a big deal of the fact that Mary had "another one." Mary played along: "And I have ANOTHER ONE at home."

The second we were safely outside and out of view, Mary erupted into laughter. I laughed, too, but only tentatively, still in shock from the woman's gall and Mary's bizarro improv theater response.

"Mare," I chided, "YOU ARE NOT PREGNANT. Why didn't you just tell her it was just the shirt you were wearing?"

In fact, I already knew the answer. Many of us have bloated days; I had been asked more than once whether I was pregnant—though, in fairness to my mom, the time she hit me with the question I actually was pregnant (with Max) but didn't yet know it. One doesn't have to strain to imagine my reaction: offense, mortification, and tears tracing cartoon arcs from the far corners of my instantly bloodshot eyes.

Mary, though, was sanguine: "Meg, she was super sweet. She didn't know. I didn't want to embarrass her, so I just played along as if I was." She glanced down and regarded her empire-waist top. "May toss this shirt, though," she said.

* * *

By the time Mary arrived, late, at the Art Institute of Pittsburgh, our big sisters Karen and Jenny were already in the back of the car. Rhianna was blasting.

Every year, in the beginning of October, Mary and I would take Jenny and Karen to dinner to celebrate their very close, fall birthdays, and we would treat. Jenny and Karen were both Libras. As such, they were both beautiful, smart, and funny; they both sought to foster peace and harmony above all else; and they both preferred to operate in the background—far away from the stage and spotlight that never ceased to be a draw for Mary and me.

We had settled into our table at P. F. Chang's on the Waterfront, which had a huge Asian fusion menu with something for everyone. We were working on our first drinks, still in the "catch-up" stage of the evening. I scanned my recent memory for things worth bringing up and seized upon a post Mary had made on Facebook, of which we were both fairly heavy users.

"Hey, Mare, I love that purple dress you had on in that picture on Facebook the other day."

I knew there was going to be an issue when Mary didn't respond instantly. Instead, after a long, peevish pause, she took a sip of her drink, then sniffed, "That dress needed to be thrown in the garbage, Meg."

I was surprised by this. "Why, Mare?"

"Well, ladies," Mary said, shifting her posture into an upright storytelling position. "After work that day, I went upstairs to change for the night. All day, the dress had felt tight. You know, it's never just a dress; there's always Spanx, undergarments, whatever the hell else. Anyway, the dress had felt tight all day, and it had gotten to the point where it was unbearable, but when I tried the zipper in the back, I couldn't get it to budge."

Karen's tone was placid: "Why didn't you just ask Ryan to do it?"

"I *did* ask Ryan to do it," Mary went on. "But he was all worried about not ruining the dress. He kept saying, 'I don't want to hurt the dress; I don't want to hurt the dress.' He was trying to reason with the zipper and, like, pinch the fabric to get it to go. But there was no extra fabric to pinch! He was pinching *me*!"

"By now, I didn't care about that damn dress. I could feel the sweat dripping off my neck and hair and I needed *out*. I started yelling: 'GET ME OUT OF THIS FUCKING DRESS!' Ryan was trying to be helpful in the way that men can. It's sweet, but it's also, like, how fucking clueless can you be? I just said I don't care about the dress, so why are you still messing with the damn zipper? Finally, I was like, 'OH JESUS, CUT IT OFF NOW! CUT IT!'"

"You'd think that would be pretty clear, but Ryan looked all confused. I don't know what part he didn't understand. What else are you going to cut it with? A samurai sword? Find some frickin' scissors; it's not rocket science."

Mary took a sip of her drink.

"So," Jenny said. "Did he cut it?"

"He finally pulled the zipper so hard that it worked, but I wish he had cut it. Never wearing it again, Jen. That dress is DEAD to me."

Mary was so animated in telling the story that we were all laughing to the point of tears, along with our waitress, some of the circling staff, and another table of ladies who basically ended up pushing their table against ours and even taking selfies with us at the end of the night.

Mary was never just a part of the party. She *was* the damn party.

p.s. When you read your fortune cookies at P. F. Chang's, always add "in bed" at the end just for fun.

19. "CHARACTER" SLIP / FASHIONABLY LATE

We were walking across the Smithfield Street Bridge. It was after work on a Friday, and our friend and former "musketeer" from our Point Park days, E. Clayton "Clay" Cornelious, was in town from New York. This necessitated a happy-hour meetup. Houlihan's, at Station Square, had half-priced appetizers and an amazing create-your-own-martini sampler. It would be a rare treat for us.

We were hobbling on inappropriate footwear. Though I almost always brought tennis shoes or flats to work to walk through town, I had forgotten on this day, probably because I cared most about putting my best "foot" forward for my friend. For her part, Mary was wearing character shoes. Usually reserved for theater and dance, the shoes are surprisingly comfortable despite the fact that they have a one- or two-inch heel, and they're typically found in only two colors, black or tan, with a strap that crosses at the ankle. Designed for flexibility, they look like bad Mary Janes with an odd, low heel—the whole point is that they "blend in."

It being Pittsburgh, there had been intermittent rain all afternoon. As we made our way in small, penguin steps across the slippy-ass Station Square sidewalk, I was giving Mary a hard time about her shoe selection: "It's just kind of odd, Mare," I said. "What's the word? 'Incongruous?'"

"Incongru-who?"

"You know, it's like that 'Sesame Street' song 'One of These Things Is Not Like the Other.' From the shins up, you're 'dressed for success,' but your shoes look like you're auditioning for an ensemble part in 'Godspell.'"

"Sometimes function before fashion is best," Mary said.

"I can't believe you, of all people, are saying this, Mare," I said.

"Seriously, Meg," Mary said. "I'm gonna end up picking you up when you slip."

In fact, Mary didn't have a chance to finish her sentence. Right before "slip" could escape her lips, she did a cartoon wipeout: Her "character shoes," feet still in them, flew high into the air and she landed hard on her posterior.

Once we both knew Mary was okay, we erupted into laughter.

The timing of Mary telling me I would slip, and then Mary herself actually slipping, was itself not a slip but clearly a gift from the gods.

For years after this, whenever I told the story, Mary would cut in: "Why in the fuck was I wearing character shoes anyway? Why did you let me, Meg?"

As though Mary took any fashion advice from me, ever.

* * *

Another time, Clay was in town, this time for a show at the Benedum Center. He and Mary were supposed to pick me up so we could meet up with some of our friends with The Heritage Players—specifically one of my best friends, Steve Gallagher. Because I always hoped that Mary would actually arrive "on time," I was all dressed up and ready to go, sitting in my living room by the front door. One hour passed. An hour and a half. I started to get texts from concerned friends.

Finally Mary and Clay picked me up.

On the way to the bar, I expressed my concerns: "Mare, we're really late. By the time we get there, our friends are going to be gone!"

Mary was dismissive: "Meg, you need to go to more parties. We don't need to be the first ones there! Haven't you heard of being 'fashionably late'?"

When we pulled up to the bar, I unbuckled my seat belt and grabbed my purse—time was of the essence! But Mary and Clay just stayed put.

"Are you coming?" I said.

"Meg," Mary said. "Just go in; we'll meet you inside."

"Uh, am I missing something?" I said.

"We need a few minutes to get into the right state of mind," Mary said.

At the time, Mary smoked cannabis periodically, mostly at "family fun day" parties around her neighborhood. She knew not to include me. For my part, I was, and am, spacey enough without THC. A glass of wine brings a nice release. Weed is a wildcard, and "giggle fit," "paranoid," or "passed out" Megan is not who I want to be.

Mary, though, was different. Not only could she handle smoking (after some misadventures in the past), but she seemed to think that cannabis brought her to a place of serenity, more or less. As Mary's life grew harder and more complicated, she would seek out her cannabis zen more and more often. This resulted in a new level of lateness. Whereas before, Mary would have been a half-hour late to pick me up, now she was often an hour late or more. I did not and do not judge.

Still, in two lives that converged in so many ways, this was one point of divergence. And, if you think of life as a kind of "if/then" flow chart—with each decision resulting in its own, cascading series of choices, each with its own consequences—you can see how divergence begets divergence, and people and relationships change.

We are not powerless in this movement apart: We can take steps to bring our paths into closer alignment, into something like convergence, and life events—both positive and negative—have a way of doing some of that work for us. The keyword is "work." If, when we are young, family and friendship are handed to us, in adulthood, those relationships require intentionality and effort. I don't see this as a negative: Our bonds are transfigured by the acts of love required to keep them healthy and strong.

Was I pissed off at Mary and Clay? Yes. Not only was I two hours late to the party, but I had to suffer the indignity of entering alone—as though I was solely responsible for my tardiness.

When, at last, the door swung open, and Mary and Clay appeared, smiling and up for the hang, I had a choice to make: I could lash out at my friends, hold a quiet grudge, or draw on my deep well of love and forgive them. I felt the warmth and affection rising within me even before I spoke.

"Finally," I said. "The party has arrived!"

20. OUR BOYS

On our second year of taking a combined family vacation to Myrtle Beach, Steve and Ryan decided to take Michaela and Kennedy on a fishing boat excursion. It was one of those "kill two birds with one stone" propositions—have an adventure and entertain the easier, older kids—only with fish (if all went well).

Mary and I were on "Team Max and Daunte" for the entire day. In reality, this wasn't so bad. Daunte is almost exactly a year and a half younger than Max, and the two have been best friends from the jump. It's remarkable: Daunte has the patience for Max, gets a kick out of him, and they just click. The Max-Daunte friendship is particularly important because Max doesn't warm to everyone.

* * *

Since early childhood, Max has gone his own way. Even prior to preschool, though Max's speech was off the charts, there were some areas of worry for me: Max was inconsolable when he was upset, and when he was excited or anxious, he would flap his hands in a way that did not seem typical. When I received a note from Max's preschool teacher listing of the same concerns, alarm bells went off in my head.

Max tested out of an "actual" autism diagnosis. Instead, he was diagnosed as having severe ADHD and "social (pragmatic) communication disorder (SCD)." According to the American Psychiatric Diagnostic and Statistical Manuals, SCD is characterized by a persistent difficulty with verbal and nonverbal communication that does not correlate with low cognitive ability. Symptoms may include "difficulty in the acquisition and use of spoken and written language," along with problems with responding appropriately in conversation.

In some areas of Max's development, he is truly eons ahead of his peers (and even his parents), but many things that neurotypical people take for granted can be challenging for my son. Max is very opinionated, and he always tells whoever he's talking to exactly what he's thinking. It can sometimes be awkward and embarrassing, but at least you know he is always honest. Max also likes routine and for things to be consistent, even constant, and he is intolerant of change. Once, I got highlights in my strawberry blonde hair—in retrospect, a terrible idea. Max was unequivocal: "Mom: I hate it."

"Aunt Mare" had a way of making Max relax, be fun, and not take himself so seriously. She also didn't take his shit or what she saw as his "quirky little meltdowns." If Max was mean to me, she would let him know: "Oh no, Maxwell Grant, you are not going to talk to your mom like that. She is my best friend; I had her first!" Max respected Mary and only challenged her when he literally couldn't help it.

* * *

At Myrtle Beach, the upside of the "Mothers and Sons Day" arrangement was that Max and Daunte were thick as thieves and Daunte's presence had a soothing effect on Max. The downside was that, as young boys, they needed to be constantly entertained. We took them to a local fair with rides and let them design their own hats, even though the styles they chose drooped over their eyes to the point where they actually couldn't see. After dinner, we went back to the condo. With no sign of the dads or girls, we went "night swimming" in the pool by the condo complex.

At the time, Max had developed an enthusiasm for turtles and frogs. Every other book I read him included a story about a damn turtle.

So, the boys were flopping around in the pool. Although Mary had her hair wrapped tightly for protection, she was not at ease with all the splashing around—she had maneuvered herself well away from the splash zone. All of a sudden, she started pointing with great urgency into the water a few feet ahead of her as though a barracuda had just swum past.

"Max! Max!" Mary whispered. "Get over here quick!"

"What, Aunt Mary?" Max said.

"Quick, Max! Over here! Now!"

More urgent pointing.

We all gathered around her, expecting something unusual or grotesque like a newt or a stranded palmetto bug. Instead, Mary was pointing to a tiny frog that was trying desperately to swim away from the black hole of the water filter.

"Max, don't you love frogs?" Mary whispered. "Buddy, you need to save him! He is struggling! Help Aunt Mare rescue this poor little guy!"

Max was all in. The frog proved resistant to being picked up, so Max used his face mask to scoop the amphibian up and deposit it gently on the dry land of the patio.

Max was the hero, and Mary would never let him forget it: "Project Save Kermit" would be a favorite topic of Mary's for the rest of her life. Whenever Mary needed to draw Max back into a conversation, she would egg him on, "Max, how did you save that frog again? What did you do?" Max would gleefully tell the tale.

* * *

Later that same summer, Mary and I were having a "ladies night" at my house. Our daughters had other plans, and Daunte and Max were upstairs in Max's room. Mary and I were drinking wine and snacking on pizza and SkinnyPop. The dads were in Steve's basement "man cave," where he had begun to spend more and more of his time.

Out of nowhere, we heard a blood-curdling scream and a crash.

Mary and I rushed to the scene, only to find Max beneath a white laundry basket at the bottom of the stairs, crying. A few feet away, Daunte lingered sheepishly. I extracted Max from the basket, looked him over, and helped him calm down. He was shaken but fine.

Mary cut to the chase: "What the heck happened, guys?"

Max gave us the straight dope: "We made a ride out of the basket, and Daunte helped me go down the steps in it!"

"Brilliant, Max," I said.

Mary turned to Daunte, apoplectic: "Really, Daunte? How are you going to push your best friend down the steps in a laundry basket? Bet you don't wanna go next, do you?"

Adorable Daunte, with Mary's big, espresso eyes and Ryan's curly hair, seemed to be trying to vanish into the living room.

"Jesus," Mary sighed. "Pray for these boys."

We invited the kids into the dining room for pizza and hung out the rest of the night as a mother-son crew.

* * *

Here's a final Max and Daunte tale: We were all at a birthday party for Daunte at the Blocher house. Max was nine and Daunte was turning eight. Max was not wild about sleepovers—they took him out of his routine and comfort zone. Rather than excluding Max, Mary and I decided that it would be a "double date" sleepover: I would stay over and hang with Mary—that way I'd be there if there was an issue. We would give the boys, and ourselves, freedom and hang out in different spaces. I would be there in a strictly "In Case of Emergency, Break Glass" capacity, enjoying a night with my best friend.

The night went great: Max had no problems, in part because he had such a healthy relationship with Daunte. The next morning, I was sitting with Max as he enjoyed the near-universal Breakfast of Sleepovers: donuts and orange juice.

Having lived with Mary, I knew that she wrapped her hair at night to prevent snagging and to keep it fresh for the next day. Mary would carefully remove all her makeup and apply lotion to her face. I also knew that, in off hours, Mary's glasses would come out. Though this version of Mary was every bit as beautiful as "public" Mary, it was decidedly not her usual "glam."

So, in her silk nightgown, "renew and revitalize" Aunt Mare descended the stairs. Max was transfixed. Slowly, he lowered the donut he was holding and stared, mouth agog, at Aunt Mare. I had no idea what was coming, but I knew it was going to be something "unfiltered." I waited.

"Um, Aunt Mare," Max began. "Are you done?"

Mary paused in midstep. "What do you mean, 'done,' Max?" Mary said.

"You usually look very beautiful," Max said. "But you have that head thing, and your face looks weird, so are you done? Are you going to fix it?"

I was mortified. One of my foibles is that I am very sensitive to any kind of commentary about my appearance, regardless of its source. If Mary's and my roles were reversed, I would have been reduced to a flood of tears.

With an actor's self-command, Mary held her position at the bottom of the stairs and didn't move a tendon on her face. A long time seemed to pass. Then she erupted into a peal of her trademark cackle. "Oh, I'm gonna fix it all right,

Max, just you wait! Aunt Mare is gonna fix the heck out of this getup, don't you worry your little heart one second about that!" More laughter. Daunte and I were now laughing, too.

Relieved, maybe, Max stood and hugged Mary, and she returned his embrace. The moment, a summation of the one-of-a-kind, quirky love they shared, was so sweet that I wanted to go in for a hug myself. In retrospect, I should have.

21. DON JOHNSON: SOLDIER FOR CHRIST

The day after Thanksgiving, Steve's extended family would split by gender. The men would hunt at camp, and the women, the "gatherers," would shop. Black Friday shopping was a significant part of the Mitchell women's Thanksgiving ritual, with its own order and customs. After the dinner, dishes, dessert, and wine, they would sit around the dining room table, spread out the circulars from the massive advertising supplement to the paper, and plot their shopping route. It was fun to be included.

My beautiful sister-in-law Tammy had picked me up very early this Friday morning. Our first stop was Target. We met with the other ladies outside of the store, walked in together, then split up to check the items off each of our individual lists. I was by the dollar items, nearing the checkout, when my phone started ringing. I assumed it was a lost shopper from our party, but it turned out to be Mary.

I could barely understand her through the tears and sobs: “Meg, MY DAD! He fucking passed away THANKSGIVING NIGHT! Oh my God, Meg, my dad; MY DAD! I’m an orphan: I have no parents now!”

“Oh God,” I said. “Mary? Mary?”

It was clear that she was in no condition to talk.

I let Tammy know what had happened, then, hands shaking, checked out and sped out to Clairton to be with my best friend. She was beyond distraught; as I held her, she went to liquid in my arms.

I had known “Mr. J” for almost as long as I’d known Mary. Mr. and Mrs. Johnson had met when they were only eighteen and eloped shortly thereafter. As a younger man, Mr. J served in the Korean War and logged time as lead singer of a band, performing around Pittsburgh and the Mon Valley.

As with any couple that stays together for more than fifty years, Mr. and Mrs. Johnson went through several phases of their partnership, but a turning point was their being "saved" just before they had Mary, who was years younger than her siblings. Accepting Jesus Christ as their Lord and Personal Savior meant that the music would be saved for church—one of several places Mary encountered it through her deeply musical family—but the bickering that is a part of married life was still totally in play:

Mr. J: "Hey Mar, this soup is a little bland today. Someone forgot the seasoning!"

Mrs. J: "Hey Don, you'd better just . . ." (stopped there).

By the time I met Mr. Johnson, he was retired, serving as an associate pastor at the church that was a central part of his life: "Don Johnson: Soldier for Christ!" He passed much of his downtime in the living room of the charming, ranch-style house in which he and Mrs. Johnson had raised their family. His "go-to" was his overstuffed recliner, where he would lounge, wrapped in a blue "Snuggy" and watch TV (*American Idol* was one of his favorites).

As with Mary and Karen, Mr. J. was diabetic, but, even when he started dialysis, he had pep in his step and spirit in his soul. After Mrs. J's passing in 2010, though, Mr. J lost some of his famous fighting spirit. Without his soulmate, wife, and best friend, Mr. J wasn't the same person. His children and grandchildren loved him intensely, and he loved them right back. Still, I will always believe Mr. J died, just shy of two years after the passing of his beloved Marlene, of a broken heart.

Every girl needs her father. They are our protectors and our first loves—if the relationship is a good one, as it had been for Mary.

As we passed from Thanksgiving into what was supposed to be the most festive time of year, Mary struggled. She was an intensely strong person, and I felt privileged to be someone with whom she would let herself be soft and vulnerable. As I did in her, Mary had faith that I would have her back, always. I stayed by her side through the viewing, the funeral, through the first Christmas season without either of her parents.

Mary would never stop grieving the loss of her parents and of her sparkling clean, womb-like childhood home that always seemed to smell of soup and seasoning. As time passed, we spent more holidays together, our already mixed families merging into a combined whole.

Despite appearances to the contrary, this new normal, too, would be ephemeral. Neither Mary nor I could imagine the ways our lives would change in the coming years, and the trials that would shake us to our cores. Best to imagine us living, as we always tried to, in the moment: Everyone cranky-ass full after a big holiday meal—except Max, who only ever committed to one biscuit, a tiny piece of turkey, and a cookie—surrounded by love, with Mr. and Mrs. J looking down from heaven, nodding approvingly.

22. GOING BACK TO CALI

When Mary and I arrived at Katie's apartment in Sunset Plaza, her five-year-old daughter, my beautiful niece Mia, met us at the door with a bottle of champagne, followed close by a barking Chihuahua. Things had changed for Katie, who had gone from working as an assistant at Dolce & Gabbana to a job as a PR rep for up-and-coming artists and filmmakers. And there was Mia, born just a few months after Max in 2008, already whip-smart and talkative, and Honey, her canine sidekick, never more than a few feet away.

"You both look beautiful," Katie said as she greeted us. "Tired, but beautiful. Mia's going to give you the tour, then you can freshen up in your bedroom."

Katie's new digs were impressive: A two-bedroom apartment a stone's throw away from West Hollywood with a balcony off the living room, original art on the walls, and a main-bedroom suite with a jacuzzi. Ever the gracious host, Katie insisted on giving up her California king–sized bed, which gave Mary and me plenty of room to stretch out (if, unfortunately, no quarters for escaping Mary's snores).

Though, as usual, this was a trip we couldn't really afford, we had come to escape the grind of life, to see our friend Clay in a touring production of *Sister Act*, and to log time with Katie and Mia (and Honey). Katie, as always, showed love through action: We were constantly on the move, whisked from boutique to fancy, IYKYK "reservations only" restaurants, to cocktail lounges, to clubs. I shared much of the "all ages" parts of the visit with Mia, who was an absolute pleasure, with a huge imagination and a well-honed wit, sharp enough to catch even "Aunt Mare" off guard.

Katie was a talker in the mold of our Nanny, the matriarch of my dad's family, who, armed with a pack of cigarettes and a Diet Coke, could hold court for hours. Though, as always, she was cagey about her personal life, Katie knew few other conversational boundaries. Our various rides around LA blurred into an oft-amusing, ongoing commentary from Katie about people she knew, family members, and, inevitably, Mary and me.

"You both should move to LA . . . I can help get you discovered . . . Mary, you have the most beautiful voice I have ever heard; you need a record deal . . . Pro-tip: Smoothies. I'm juicing for life . . . We need to get mom out of her damn 'chair' . . . Mo, you have an 'at risk' chin . . . Mo, I can see you doing comedy, maybe on TV . . . Oh my God, Mo, your bras and panties—I can't even. Not cute enough! Pro-tip: If you don't feel sexy underneath, how can you project 'sexy' to the world? . . . I know the best lingerie store . . . Do you think we should get mom a personal trainer? . . . Mare, your hair looks amazing; Mo, if you lived in LA, I would get you the most beautiful hair extensions . . . You both need to move to LA ASAP; you're still young enough to be able to lie about your age, but time is running out! . . . Mare, be glad you're a year younger than Megan. Thirty-nine, holy shit! . . . You both look great, but we need to get you some anti-aging cream!"

Anytime we went anywhere, we would be met by Katie's friends—many of them, from what I could tell, around my age. Katie would proudly introduce Mary and me to each new person. Her introductions were often generous to the point of stretching the truth: Mary and I would be billed as "actors" (no mention of our day jobs) who had performed in productions "around the Northeast." While this last point was not exactly a lie, the conflation of "Pittsburgh and its southeast suburbs" with a nine-state region felt a touch deceptive—but why not? What Katie said in LA would stay in LA.

More problematic, for me, were the attentions of Mary and Katie. Mary and Clay's relationship had "evolved" from two-thirds of the three amigos into something more personal, off limits even to me as Mary's bestie. On this particular evening, at the W Hollywood, Mary and Clay had gotten into an argument, and each had stormed off in a different direction. Katie, meanwhile, was fully immersed in her LA friend world, talking about people and places I didn't know, taking selfies with various of her gathered friends. I just wanted to have time to sit and talk to my sister. I started to feel jealous.

What does a sister do when she feels spurned? Well, this sister started drinking on an empty stomach. Before long, I had far surpassed my (admittedly not very high) "Meg limit." In search of a change of pace, more than anything, I headed to the bathroom—where, it turned out, Mary was working through her anger at Clay. Her attention shifted to me, a caricature of a dejected, sulking sibling: shoulders rounded, lips downturned, eyes welled with deeply felt, alcohol-fortified hurt.

"Meg, oh my God, you look crumpled; did Katie say something?"

Even when you try to whisper in a public restroom, there is amplification, echo; I didn't care.

"I miss my sister, Mare," I said. "I feel like I came all this way to see her, but, like, she's more interested in her friends than in spending time with me."

"I don't know, Meg," Mary said. "Katie really loves you a lot. Think of all the ways she's shown love. She gave up her bed. The bottle of champagne."

"The 'pro-tips,'" I said, and we both laughed. But my mood lingered in the melancholy zone.

"The one way Katie *hasn't* shown love," I said, "is by taking the time to really talk to me. I mean, *actually* talk to me. I'm not talking about pro-tips."

"She just wants to impress you, Meg," Mary said. "You're her big sis; she wants to show you how happy and successful she is in LA."

"I don't want to be impressed," I said. "I mean, of course, I'm impressed. She moved out here when she was twenty-two, and she's built this whole life for herself. But she doesn't have to prove anything to me. I'd love her the same amount if she'd stayed in Pittsburgh. I just want her to be my sister."

Mary sighed, then screwed up her face into a look of contemplation. "Meg," she said. "Honesty is the best approach—my dad used to say, 'To our loved ones we must promise, in the hardest times to be honest.'" Mary paused. "You're sisters, for fuck's sake. Go tell Katie why you're upset. You got this, girl. Go!"

Propelled by Mary's pep talk and liquid courage, I made my way back into the restaurant to find Katie. She was on the stairs, taking "stair selfies" with her "replacement me."

"Katie," I began. "Can I talk to you alone for a second?"

We rounded the corner into the corridor leading to the bathrooms.

"What's up, Mo?" Katie asked, as if she were inquiring as to the time.

"You've been super generous," I said. "I really appreciate everything you've done for Mary and me."

Katie's eyes assumed the glazed-over look of someone listening to a confirmation voicemail from a dentist's office.

In an effort to boost initiative, I cleared my throat, then tried again: "I love you, Katie, but I just kind of feel like you aren't making time for me. Everywhere we go, there's, like, ten other people, and you're always more interested in talking to them than me."

Katie wasn't the sort of person to show contrition directly. Instead, like a pit bull scolded by someone other than its owner, Katie would go on the attack. Rather than canines and crushing jaws, Katie's weapon was language, which she wielded like a switchblade in the hands of one of the Sharks in *West Side Story*.

"You've always been ungrateful, Megan. The last time you came here, I moved my life around for you, made everything about you, showed you the best of everything, and you made me feel guilty for going on a single fucking date. This time, I knew I couldn't do anything without you because you would complain and make me feel bad, so I decided to bring you with me."

"You're not on a *date,* Katie," I said.

"No," Katie snorted. "But I'm living my life. And this is *my* life and I brought you into it. I've taken you to the best stores, the finest restaurants, and the most exclusive clubs in LA. If it weren't for me, you'd be taking pictures of stars on the Hollywood Walk of Fame or riding King Kong 360 3-D at Universal fucking Studios." She narrowed her eyes in angry contemplation. "Actually, you wouldn't even be doing that. You wouldn't even be in LA; the only reason you're even here is me. I have stopped everything to be the best, most generous host I know how to be. I have brought you everywhere. And you have the gall to pull me away from my friend and shit on me and make me feel bad." She opened her eyes wide for full effect. "Fuck you."

And, with that, Katie swaggered away.

It was as though Katie's words were a bucket of water and I was the Wicked Witch of the West: alone in some hallway in a fancy Hollywood hotel, I could feel myself melting into a puddle of makeup and tears. I made my way woozily to the bathroom, where Mary had seemingly taken up residency.

"Oh no," she said as she saw me slink in. "That didn't go well!"

The presence of a sympathetic figure, in this case, was like water on a grease fire. I was literally making "boo hoo hoo" sounds when one of the bathroom attendants jumped in to console me: "Ah girl, I have a sister, too."

"Oh, thanks," I sniffed. "I appreciate it."

The attendant lingered. "My mom used to say, about me and my sister, 'No one gets her like her sister.'"

"I like how it goes both ways," Mary said.

"Oh, it *definitely* went both ways with us."

Mary escorted me back to the bar area. We had tried to work makeup miracles in the bathroom, but my eyes were puffy and I had the dazed look of someone no longer buzzed but not yet hungover.

I had given up on the rest of the evening: There was no way to recover from getting screamed at in public by your little sister. Mary would order me a "comedown" drink, and I'd nurse it, and either Katie would come and find us and take us home or—well, that was the only option, inconceivable as it seemed to be.

As we approached the bar, I noticed someone I recognized—but from where? Short-ish. The round eyes. The glasses. The fedora.

"Oh my God, Mare! It's will.i.am from the Black Eyed Peas!"

"Meg," Mare said. "Your damn eyes are blurry from crying; that's not will . . . "

And then there we were, face to face with the man who had once proclaimed to the world, "I got a feeling / That tonight's gonna be a good night!"

Mary needed confirmation. "Wait," she said, squinting her eyes. "Are you will.i.am?"

"Yeah," the man himself said, with a warm, lived-in tone that suggested this was not the first time he had fielded such a question. Across the bar, the other "Peas" became evident.

The whole thing felt like a dream. Neither Mary nor I could manage to say anything more sensible than "Oh my God." An expert with situations like this, will.i.am suggested a selfie. Though I looked like someone whose night had been much more "boom boom pow" than a "good good night," who was I to say no?

Katie did later track Mary and I down. It was not her way to apologize; instead, she would buy you a drink or offer you a cigarette—she smoked when she was out—and steer the conversation into safer ground.

That night, the three of us sat by the hotel pool as Katie and I smoked cigarette after cigarette. Katie pretty much monologued, regaling Mary and me with stories about dating a cage fighter—she had always had a thing for bad boys—and about a mysterious contact she had in the Bay Area who helped her out with money sometimes when she needed it.

The truth is that all of this seemed distant, even obscure to me, and given the late hour and everything we'd been through, I had a hard time keeping track of the names and information. The point was that Katie's life was chock full of characters and intrigue, which seemed fitting for the sister who had always longed for a glamorous, complicated life away from the hills of Southwest Pennsylvania. In college, Mary and I had hosted a glamour party; Katie's whole life was a glamour party. It was not for me to say whether that was good or bad—I could only observe that this was an achievement for Katie, the fulfillment of a dream.

The next day was my birthday. My eyes were still so swollen that I had to wear Jackie O–style witness protection sunglasses. We had brunch at the Sur with Mia, and Mary won an impromptu singing competition at the House of Blues. Later, while Mary performed emergency surgery on a painful hangnail, I got to visit with three of my cousins. Mary had mentioned wanting a butterfly tattoo; Katie made that happen and planned a very indulgent birthday dinner for me to boot.

At the Sur, Mary, Katie, and I posed for a picture that lingers in my memory. Mary and I, to Katie's right and left, are both clad in black—not standard "brunchware," but the Sur was not Applebee's, so we had dressed it up for the occasion. Katie, her hair parted in the middle, her sleep-deprived eyes hidden behind a pair of Gloria Steinem aviators, is rocking a form-fitting red tank-top and tight blue jeans, her arms wrapped around Mary and me. At the center of the table is a bouquet of bright roses.

I like to think that, somewhere in the time-space continuum, this hug continues in perpetuity. Mary and Katie were both so strong, so driven, so rooted in action. Words mattered to them, and both could wield language mercilessly in a fight, but what mattered more was *doing*. The acts of kindness and generosity

Mary and Katie regularly showed to the people they cared about most, including me, were seldom short of uplifting and astounding. I was so inspired, so buoyed, by their love and care. They, in turn, shared a mutual respect and love for each other.

Back in 2013, no one could have foreseen that, in less than ten years, both Mary and Katie would be gone. How I wish, even now, I could go back in time and yell, "Stop!" Maybe if Katie had kept her arms around us, maybe if Mary and I had never left LA, if that final moment could have been stretched into infinity, the ending could have been different—or nonexistent—and their heroic love would persist in the world, and not just in the hearts of those whose lives they touched so deeply. Maybe Mare and I would be planning another trip to LA for this year (I have a big birthday coming up). Katie, Mia, deep into her teens, and Honey the Chihuahua would greet us at the door.

"You look beautiful," Katie would say. "Tired, but beautiful."

ACT 3: SPIRIT SISTERS

1. SUNSET SISTER

In the very early hours of February 2, 2016, I received a bizarre Facebook Messenger text from a friend of Katie's named Karen. We had never officially met, so this was scary. Karen explained that she was Katie's neighbor, that Katie had been sick, and that she had taken her to the hospital. The doctors wanted to know from Katie's family and friends the last time Katie had been "lucid." They were thinking that my little sister, still a month and change from her thirty-fifth birthday, had suffered a stroke shortly after neck manipulation at the chiropractor.

Karen was shaken; I could tell from carefully chosen words, and from the gaps between those words, that the situation was serious. I told her that Katie had called my parents earlier that evening in tears, complaining of a headache. My parents had told her to go to the hospital. Katie wasn't a crier; we knew that she had been complaining about a sore neck, but the details were hazy. I had sent Katie a text the previous day, February 1st, to check on her but I hadn't heard back. She had mentioned something on social media about "pinching a nerve."

Though I knew instinctively that I could trust Karen, my first reaction was denial. "Oh my God," I said. "What the fuck? My sister is healthy. She's thirty-four years old. This has to be some kind of mistake."

Karen, bravely, filled in as many of the blanks as she could. Katie had called saying she had to go to the hospital. Karen hurried over. Katie was having a hard time moving one side of her body. Karen had wrapped Katie's good arm over her shoulders and helped her to the car. On the ride to Cedars Sinai, one side of Katie's face had gone numb. They had checked in at the emergency room, but Katie hadn't been admitted. Katie could barely sit up in her chair. She vomited, screamed. Finally, they admitted her. The doctors told Katie she was having a stroke. They put her in a reclined position and gave her blood thinners. She was something like lucid again but deeply upset. They said they needed to take her to surgery. She pleaded with them not to take her.

There was a story in the news recently about a woman in Texas who was mowing the lawn, away from any trees, when a snake fell out of the clear blue sky, wrapped itself around her arm, and began hissing and lunging at her eyes. Before the woman could extricate herself, a brown-shouldered hawk dive-bombed her and sunk its talons into her arm in an effort to extract the snake. The story captures well the lightning-quick speed with which terror can descend upon us, interrupting and altering, sometimes permanently, the course of our otherwise ordinarily proceeding lives. Katie was fine, and then she was not. My life was normal-seeming, and then it was not.

In bed, with sleeping Max by my side, my mind raced. People pinch nerves in their neck all the time; I feel like I have a pinched nerve somewhere in my body more often than not. How the fuck could a pinched nerve and a trip to the chiropractor result in a stroke? Just the word *stroke* felt like something out of a nightmare. Old people had strokes; little sisters in their mid-thirties did not. It was that simple.

I reached out to my support system. Steve was away on a business trip. I called my friend

Steve because we had been messaging that evening. He was supportive. I was hesitant to phone Mary because it was the middle of the night—but I needed my best friend.

As she always did, Mary picked up, and before she could ask why I was calling, I broke down: "Oh my God, Mary. Not my sister. This can't be happening. This can't be happening. She had a STROKE? How the fuck could she have a STROKE? What is happening? This cannot be real. Mare, Mare, tell me this is a dream."

Mary was groggy; it took her a minute or two to put together what I was saying: "Slow down, Meg. It's gonna be okay. Slow down. I'm here for you."

"A fucking STROKE, Mare! She's thirty-four!"

"There are different kinds of strokes," Mary said.

"People die from strokes!" I said.

"Katie is young," Mary said. "But, Meg, you need to rewind. I still don't get what the hell you're talking about."

When, finally, Mary was able to assemble the facts, the chronology, she went into "reassuring" mode. "Meg," she said. "Seriously, Katie is a badass. She will beat whatever this is. I know it.

Your sister is a badass. If anyone on earth can beat this, it is your sister. I know it."

I held my tongue. The truth was that I wasn't sure of anything.

Morning always comes, for better or for worse. I got the kids off to school and waited for notifications from my phone. Information was slow to trickle in. My parents, making their way across the country, an act of sheer courage for them, were incommunicado.

Things in my life had been hard. On Jenny's birthday, September 29, I had been laid off from my position at the Art Institute of Pittsburgh. It had never been an easy or particularly well-paying job, but it was security, community—and then it was gone. Steve and I were still sorting through Max's diagnosis and what it would mean for him and our family. We would always love each other, but there was increasing tension, and distance, between us. I had been interviewing for jobs sporadically, focusing on my kids, acting on the side—holding it together, but barely. And then, from the ether, like a snake dropped out of the sky, this.

Why did bad things happen? I didn't know, and I still don't. Catholics are taught to have faith, period. Further questioning is seen as, if not blasphemous, not "staying in one's lane" with God. Who are *we* to wonder why? Instead I bargained, begged: "Oh God, please let this turn out all right! Let my sister be okay! Oh God, please oh please let my baby sister be okay!"

In midmorning, Karen wrote again via Facebook. Katie had been brought out of surgery into the Neuroscience Critical Care Unit (NCCU). At first she was herself, able to talk; the doctor emphasized that Katie would need to take Aspirin pills to thin her blood for the rest of her life. Ten minutes passed, twenty. Katie grew silent, still. The doctors ran some tests, conferred, then confirmed that Katie had passed into locked-in syndrome. She was conscious, awake, but unable to move or speak. She could move her eyes up and down and blink, that was all.

The doctors explained that one blink would mean "no," and two would mean "yes." Did Katie understand? Two blinks. Did she know where she was? Two blinks. Could she move? One blink. Was she in pain? Two blinks. Again, was she in pain? Two blinks. The doctors conferred and then took her away again. To the extent that there was a "positive," Katie had been responsive, and her breathing had been steady. Only time would tell whether her condition would improve.

I was in constant communication with Jenny and Mary. In retrospect, it's easy to think, "Why didn't you just drive straight to the airport," but it was impossible to know, with the second hand information we had, what we were looking at. Moreover, Jenny and I both had young children, and such a flight would cost hundreds of dollars, so we couldn't just up and take a redeye to LA.

Katie's dear friend Matt had reached out with a question. Katie didn't need to be intubated, yet, but if that was necessary, would it be okay? I said yes but asked him to call my brother Stephen. Why hadn't I heard from my parents? Looking back, now, the answer is obvious; at the time, though, I was desperate for an explanation from someone in the family about what the fuck was going on.

Mary left work early, drove straight through the inky February evening to my house, and, on sight, hugged me, held me, tried to calm me. Though I'd been losing my composure all day, I lost it once again in Mary's sisterly embrace. "My sister, Mare," I sobbed. "Oh, God, not my sister!"

"I know, Meg," Mary said into my hair as she patted my back. "I know; I got you."

Mary had a plan, cute in retrospect. She straightened me up, dusted off my shoulders. "You've just been looking at your phone all day," she said. "We need to get you to one of your happy places. We're going to Applebee's."

I laughed for the first time all day. "What?"

"You need a glass of wine," Mary said. "And some of that shrimp salad."

"The wine for damn sure," I said.

"Meg," Mary said. "That shrimp salad is your fave."

"We'll see," I said.

"Hell yes, we will."

The scene at the restaurant was surreal: The whole place was designed to feel familiar and comfortable, but, in my current state, all I could feel was dissonance. Everyone was just going about their lives as though nothing had happened. For the waitstaff, for the people in the booths eating riblets and mozzarella sticks, sipping cocktails, it was a regular fucking Tuesday evening. Meanwhile, my sister's life—my life—hung in the balance.

I nursed a glass of white wine; I couldn't bring myself to eat any of the Thai shrimp salad I had ordered at Mary's insistence.

"Meg," Mary kept saying. "I know it's going to be fine. Do you know your sister? Things are rough, no doubt. But if anyone can pull through something like this, Katie can."

I asked for a box for my food.

As we were approaching my house, my brother Stephen called. He had spoken to Matt about Katie's condition. My stomach dropped seven flights. Mary pulled over so I could listen to my brother fully. At first, I was so nervous for any updates that I was talking over him, my anxiety a fifteen out of ten. Finally, Stephen stopped me: "Meg, I need you to listen to me. Are you listening, Meg?" My brother is always honest and open, and his tone did not sound good.

I heard the word "yes" come out of my mouth before I could take it back.

"Katie is gone. The sister we knew is not there anymore. She is not going to be able to be the person we knew."

I couldn't speak to end the call; I handed the phone to Mary. The next thing from me was a guttural wail—the kind of sound heard only in slasher movies. I couldn't breathe, couldn't catch my breath; I opened the car door and vomited into the purple night.

I know from Mary's retelling that she basically moved me by my shoulders and walked me into the house. She opened the door, and I let out another scream and collapsed onto the couch. Michaela came down the stairs, alarmed by what she had heard. Mary related what Stephen had told her. Michaela started breaking down: Not her Aunt Katie, she had just been home for Christmas! We settled on the couch. Mary held one of my hands and Michaela the other. Poor Steve didn't know what to say or do; he was trying to be the voice of reason: "Meg, we don't have all the information. How can she be 'gone' if she is still alive? If she's still alive, there must be a chance . . . "

This enraged me. Stephen had talked to Matt, and Matt had been there in the hospital with the doctors. With my parents holed up somewhere in hospital hell, we would have to trust Matt. He wasn't family, but he cared deeply for Katie, and if he said that my sister would no longer be able to be the person I knew, there was no point in questioning him. Which left only the truth: Katie was gone. Oh my God, my sister was gone. Oh, God, let this be a dream!

Mary and Michaela and I held each other: A sisterhood.

The next day, the detailed "information" Steve had sought began to trickle in from my parents. A priest had given Katie the Anointing of the Sick. The bottom line was that Jenny and I needed to get to LA immediately—no small matter. Worse, I had a job interview that same afternoon, which I insisted on going to; again, in retrospect, what the fuck was I thinking? My brother-in-law, Rich, booked a flight for the two of us. Neither Jenny nor I could be described as a "quick packer," but time was of the essence: clothes, underwear, and makeup were jammed into suitcases. My sister-in-law Tammy would drive me to my interview, Steve would pick me up, and together we would pick up Jenny.

On my way to Jenny's house, another call. Katie was unresponsive; the medical term was "brain dead." Most of the time, we think of life and death as a binary: white (life) and black (death). The truth is that, in some cases, when we are on life support, our hearts are beating and our lungs are taking in air, but the "thinking" part of our mind has ceased to exist. I still struggle to accept this. How could anyone say for certain whether Katie was or wasn't thinking, or dreaming, even as she lay there unable to move? When Stephen later asked the doctors about this, they said simply, "We don't know."

Jenny and I had to make a connecting flight in Minneapolis. We had never been to the Minneapolis airport and had no idea where we were going. I didn't think to change out of my interview clothes; my heels were driving Jenny crazy as we hurried from one gate to the other. Finally, I had to take off my shoes so we could make a run for it. We flew to LA in total silence, holding hands, lost in our own thoughts.

The stories we tell ourselves about our lives give them meaning. This meaning is a big part of what sustains us when snakes fall from the sky, or worse. For me, there was my family, both immediate and extended, my friendships with Mary, Nique, and others, and, of course, theater. Work had been a thing, too, and, as a creative person I had appreciated the proximity to similarly minded people the Art Institute gave me. Now that was gone—to be replaced by I knew not what. For Jenny, who managed a prescription call bank for the University of Pittsburgh Medical Center, work occupied a more prominent role, and family was also huge.

Back in Pittsburgh, Mary was finding her way: There was friction in her relationship with Ryan that often resulted in sparks, and sometimes flames, but they remained partners. Mary was an excellent mom to Kennedy and Daunte, and she had real ambition in the world of property management. If Mary had lost some of her passion for theater, performing before an audience never failed to bring it back.

What had Katie's purpose been? Her number one goal in life was to be the best mother to her daughter, Mia, that she possibly could. This meant finding a way to provide Mia with, literally, the best of everything, from school to clothes to a laptop for homework (Mia was, at the time, only seven). Katie's second, related purpose—and this went back to when she was a little girl dancing around in our parents' front yard in Lisa Frank underwear, or unrepentantly upstaging her siblings in family photos—was to find a way to put herself out in front of other people and make them care about her. This is part of what had driven Mary early on, too—both she and Katie were ambitious, bold, babies of their respective families—but, when stardom no longer seemed imminent, Mary had changed gears. Katie, too, had shifted focus, for a time: There had been a jeans company and a few midlevel PR gigs. Still, there never could be any doubt that Katie wanted to be out in front, even if she was also the savvy businesswoman drumming up interest behind the scenes.

Katie's "big break" had emerged, almost by accident, from the ashes of her PR career. A well-paying PR job had evaporated overnight when the company was sold. Katie found herself, not for the first time in her adult life, without a dime to her name. Though she was thirty-two and stood only five feet and *maybe* one inch (she would later claim publicly to be in her midtwenties and to be 5 feet, 3 inches, LOL) Katie was not the kind of person to back down from a challenge. A few years earlier, around the time she gave birth to Mia, she had listed the following goals:

- I will have a happy and healthy child who feels loved.
- I will be financially wealthy with millions of dollars in the bank.
- I will be well-known and admired by many.

- I will wear designer clothing.
- I will travel to beautiful and luxurious places all over the world.
- I will be considered beautiful by many.
- I will have an amazing, hard body.
- I will be famous publicly.
- I will be in love and I will be loved in return by a man who is proud of me and my daughter.

Katie wasn't without privilege, but there was little family money to bankroll these dreams. What she had was herself, and she would put that resource to use. It wasn't so much that Katie aspired to be a model; Katie aspired to be rich and famous, and if that meant being a model, so be it. She was smart enough to know that social media was only just beginning to explode. She gave herself a year. She already had a robust network of contacts from her days in PR; now, she would use them to help sell herself as a brand. She posed on Instagram and Snapchat. Interspersed with the photos were inspirational quotes and found images that helped inform and shape her brand.

A photo shoot caught the eye of new LA web zine Arsenic, which led to more shoots and videos. Arsenic heads Billy Hawkins and

Amanda Micallef shared Katie's vision and drive. Their work went viral and Katie's number of followers soared from the hundreds of thousands into the millions. Katie would leverage mentions of services and products for cash or trade. Her online work crossed over into old-school magazines, as Katie modeled for Playboy, Sports Illustrated, GQ. She was crowned Queen of Snapchat.

In the very early days of influencer culture, before "influencer" was even a widely used word, Katie was an influencer of influencers. Less than a week before her stroke, Katie and Matt had launched a media blitz in promotion of Matt's new sports betting company, JetBet, in which Katie held a stake. A billboard prominently featuring Katie's rear end, fourteen feet high, towered above Sunset Boulevard. And she had finally started to make money, some of which she had invested into a total reboot of Mia's bedroom—a rosary with silver-plated beads draped over the desk lamp, the final touch. A three-panel painting was delivered to Katie's apartment a day or two after she died. Depicted was Etta James singing "Life is beautiful."

If Katie's purpose in life was to fulfill her potential as a creative person, as something of an unrepentant exhibitionist, as a businesswoman, as a sister and daughter, and, above all, as a mom to Mia, she had been well on her way before the metaphorical snake fell out of the sky.

But, while I was thinking about meaning, what purpose could the tragedy unfolding before us in real time have? Catholic doctrine says, once again, a version of "don't ask"—God will help you carry whatever crosses you must bear. I could appreciate the purity of this answer, but not its inconclusiveness. To accept suffering unquestioningly may lead to a form of knowledge, and I begrudge no one the right to forge such a relationship with God. What I wanted at this moment, however, was an answer to the question "Why?" None was forthcoming.

Katie's personal assistant Kristen Corona picked Jenny and me up at the airport. "Corona," as Katie had called her, and as we called her, was saintly but powerless to stop time or reverse it. It was already late; there was no traffic to speak of. Before Jenny and I knew it, we were parking, making our way into the hospital. Corona gave us directions to the NCCU, on the eighth floor of the Saperstein Critical Care Tower. Stephen was waiting by the elevators. He led us around the corner to Katie's room, where my mom and dad, white with exhaustion and despair, were waiting.

Katie was elevated, intubated, hooked up to myriad tubes and machines. Above her bed, a monitor tracked her blood pressure, heart rate, and oxygen level. Katie's hair, makeup, and tanning team—Olivia, Melissa, and Christina—had attended to every detail of her appearance. She looked beautiful and absolutely Katie-like: Every single hair and touch of makeup was in perfect place. If Katie's pallor had been expertly concealed, her unwavering, disconcerting stillness betrayed the heartbreaking truth of her condition.

I spoke to Katie, pleaded with her and with God to answer me; in the moment, the only answers came in the form of comically inappropriate bleeps and bloops from the life support machine.

Jenny and I shared a few private moments with Katie, and then we were joined by Katie's friend Trisha. This felt right. It would be Katie's friends and loved ones, and our own friends and family, who would get us through the nightmare that was the next few days in LA. In the early morning, Stephen, Jenny, and I took a car back to Katie's apartment, which was still exactly as she had left it, with a smoothie waiting in the refrigerator. Stephen slept, on the couch, and my dad on Mia's bed (Mia was with her adoring father, Alex, and her devoted *safta*, Hana). My mom, Jenny, and I shared Katie's California king.

The next day, after calls from TMZ, drama over a GoFundMe, discussion about organ donation, and much shepherding to make sure those closest to Katie were present, my sister was removed from life support. I held her hand as her light gently faded. My heart was shattered into a million little pieces.

My dear friend Nique and her husband Tony, fresh off a seven-hour drive from San Jose, were waiting outside Katie's place. They escorted me to say one last goodbye to Katie and retrieve her possessions at Cedars Sinai. Nique and Tony would stay by our side until we left LA.

Mary and I had been texting through it all, but it was on the phone with her, back at Katie's place, that I truly lost my shit. Mary asked how I was. I was shaking and sobbing, barely able to assemble words into cohesive thoughts or sentences. Where to start? Mia. Once again, my heart shattered into a million little pieces. We needed to be there for Mia. How would we also, somehow, attend to Katie's final arrangements, plan a memorial in a city we barely knew, and pack Katie's essential possessions into boxes? And how could we do any of those things as we grieved this sudden and soul-crushing loss? Oh, fuck, to be back at Applebee's, when there still seemed like there could be a chance. Dear God, can you just bring me back to Applebee's? "Mary," I sobbed. "What did I get?"

"The Thai shrimp salad," Mary said. "As usual."

"Give me the fucking Thai shrimp salad!"

Mary's voice assumed a soothing, motherly tone: "I got you, Meg. Mare has you."

"My sister, Mary. My baby sister. Oh God, not my little baby sister."

"She was tough, Meg."

"I know she fought; I know she did."

"She is resting, Meg. She is home with Jesus."

"I don't want her to be home with Jesus; I want her to be here with Mia. I want her to be here with me. Oh God."

A pause, then from Mary: "I need to be there with you, Meg."

"No, Mare," I protested. "You don't have the money, and things are so crazy. Thank you so much for offering to come, but you don't need to. Nique is here. My family is here."

"I need to be there for the memorial."

"We don't even know when the memorial is going to be."

"Well, let me know when you do."

"Mare, seriously."

"I *am* being serious. You are my best friend."

"You are my best friend, so hear me when I say you don't have to."

"What would you do, Meg?"

Mary had me there.

Mary was not one for idle talk, but we didn't discuss her coming until a couple of days later, in the middle of the afternoon. I honestly can't recall what I was doing because the truth is that I don't know what we did.

We learned quickly that LA people, or at least Katie's LA people, got shit done. The day after Katie died, Alex and Billy from Arsenic met and worked out the details for the memorial. It would be held at one of Alex's properties in

Beverly Hills. Arsenic would take care of the event planning, and Alex would cover the property-specific details like parking and security people, the latter just in case. Around the house, one major task was to begin sorting through Katie's things, including an entire closet full of pretty much every official paper—from tax records to parking tickets to court documents—she had ever received.

The living room was the gathering place, and it was there that an elephant from Mia's room was deployed as the talking piece; this way, no one would talk over anyone else when discussions got heated, as they sometimes did when we were navigating hard topics (and almost every topic was difficult).

When I saw that Mary was calling, my feeling was one of relief. My phone was my lifeline to the world outside Katie's apartment. There were so many people to call and text, so many details to be on top of. My bestie was my most trusted confidante: The person to whom I could vent, cry, be vulnerable without risking judgment. I moved into Katie's bathroom and closed the door.

"Mare," I said. "Things are so fucking crazy."

"They're about to get crazier," Mary said, "because I'm here."

"What do you mean 'you're here'?"

"I'm at LAX, Meg," Mary said. "Can you get someone to pick me up?"

The needle scratched off the record in my head. "Wait," I said. "What?"

"I'm in LA, but no way am I renting a car," Mary said. "Can you ask someone to drive out to pick me up?"

"I told you, Mare, you didn't have to come."

"That's not where we left it," Mary said. "Where we left it, we agreed that, if the tables were turned, you would come to me."

Of course, that wasn't where we had left it—or anyway, how I remembered we had left it, but everything was a blur and, besides, the point was moot because Mary was on the ground in LA. Another angel had come: my bestie and soulmate.

Once again, Corona, a fellow Pittsburgher, came to the rescue—the start of a close friendship that continues to endure.

When Mary arrived at Katie's apartment, Hello Kitty bag in tow, I once again lost it. Mary had moved mountains and rallied as my "person" to be there. For one of the few times in my life, I was truly speechless. Mary held me and, with a one-line response, brushed off any platitudes about heroism from the ever-present crowd of people in the apartment. "It's what besties do," Mary said.

A significant issue was that there was, literally, nowhere for Mary to sleep. My dad was still on Mia's bed, with Stephen now in the snore zone on Mia's bedroom floor. Tony was on the couch. My mom, Jenny, Nique, and I had been sharing Katie's bed. The only solution was to make it a true "clown-car bed" and find some space for Mare; we were only too happy to oblige.

In the immediate passing of a loved one, you find yourself in some truly ridiculous situations, and you get through them because you have no other choice. Indeed, the bonding moments shared by the ladies of Katie's bed—including numerous laughs about Nique's footed Superman pajamas, various people's (Mary's) snoring, night care for hair, and the need to pee—were some of the most memorable and heartwarming of our time in LA. Truly, I don't know what I, we, would have done without Nique and Mary.

Mary's contributions, naturally, extended well beyond emotional support. Her quickness and discerning eye for what to pack and what to leave were second only to those of my cousin Tracy, another angel, who made the drive up from San Diego.

On the morning of Katie's memorial, Mary was feeling mixed about her ability to sing Sarah McLachlan's "Angel" with Nique and me, and Whitney Houston's "I Will Always Love You" solo.

"Meg," Mary croaked, her hair still in a bonnet. "My voice is shit this morning; I can already tell. I think it's the air conditioning."

"Mare," I said. "Why does there always have to be drama?"

"You're asking *me* this?" Mary said.

From Katie's bathroom, I could hear Nique laughing. "Stop it you guys," she said. "We're all going to be great! We have God on our side today."

"We'll have to see," Mary said.

I lobbed a pillow at her but missed.

The memorial was beautiful and so, so hard. A succession of speakers tried to find a meaning in Katie's tragic passing, but no one quite succeeded. We were still so lost, so beside ourselves with shock and grief. Mary was, of course, in perfect form, and when she let loose to sing "I Will Always Love You," the crowd was filled with awe. Though it wasn't a religious service, Mary's and Nique's voices, both of which had gained their "wings" at church, seemed to bestow God's beautiful, ineffable blessings on the proceedings. We all found sanctuary in song.

At least one agent who had been connected to my sister handed Mary a business card for possible representation. Though Mary was past believing that performing would bring her material salvation—she was resolute that the answer would be property management and, perhaps, real estate—she proudly took the card as a memento.

In April, when my family finally had Katie's hometown memorial Mass and wake in Pittsburgh, Mary and Nique once again never left my side. They were my angels, my rocks, and literally kept me alive in the hardest days, weeks, and months of my life. They were also a grounding force for my parents and siblings, to whom they were also anointed family.

When I think about this time, my mind flashes back to the brunch that Katie, Mary, Mia and I shared at the Sur in West Hollywood, and the photo we took there: Mary to the right, me to the left, Katie in the center, her arms wrapped around us. Katie and Mary had seen each other since—Mary planned my fortieth birthday party, for which Katie flew across the country to attend. Still, the moment captured by the picture lingers, in part because it captures a moment of joy, in part because it stands testament to the fragility of life.

We never know when a snake is going to fall out of the sky and change things forever, so we must hold each other tighter, love each other more, and take nothing for granted. We must live with purpose.

2. BESTIES WHO TATTOO TOGETHER STAY TOGETHER

Mary had decided that, for my forty-second birthday (who was counting?), she would get me a tattoo. She would get herself one, too. This would be Mary's way of forcing me to do something I'd been talking, noncommittally, about doing for a long time. Specifically, I'd been talking about getting a tattoo as a way of memorializing my sister Katie.

I had settled, in theory, on a pair of angel wings, which would represent both Katie's ascension into heaven and her new role as one of my guardian angels. After her passing, Katie's voice had become a prominent part of the fabric of my mind. I could hear her passing judgment on my outfit choices, see her rolling her eyes when I did something questionable, feel her protecting me as I drove my black Hyundai ever tentatively home from rehearsals in distant suburbs well after dark.

In the picture of Katie we used on her prayer card, she stands in front of a pair of wings, her head turned and eyes shut, as if in reflection. On the reverse side was Robert Frost's "The Road Not Taken," a favorite poem of Katie's. My feeling is that Katie liked the poem because it is, in part, about the difficulty of choice. We will second guess ourselves, and we will be second guessed by a chorus of people with an incomplete grasp of the details and circumstance. It is so easy to lose perspective, to forget the facts of a situation after we make our choices, but in a real way, as we go forward, those facts cease to matter.

I was noncommittal because I had never gotten a tattoo, and because, once you got one, there was no going back. Katie herself had tried, with only partial success, to have a tattoo she'd gotten in college lasered out of existence. Tattoos may not exactly be forever, but they are about as close as anything in this life can get.

"We're *doing* it," Mary said over the phone.

"I need to think about it more," I protested.

"No, the appointment has been booked," Mary said. "We're going. I'll pick you up. Be ready!"

I had dutifully found a wallet-sized image of a pair of wings to be stamped into my skin on my right rib cage. I had gathered my courage and waited patiently at my desk at my new job at Triangle Tech, a post-secondary technical school on Perrysville Avenue, deep into the North Side.

Mary was, of course, running late. "Don't say anything," she said when I got into the car. "We'll be on time enough."

What did that even mean?

"I brought my angel," I said, and showed Mary the wallet-sized image of angel wings I'd brought for the artist.

"Meg," Mary said, glancing over. "That's tiny. That's microscopic. The tattoo guy will have to use a microscope to do that. What's the point?"

"Well," I said. "Tattoos hurt, right? So the smaller the tattoo, the less the pain?"

Mary cackled. "I'm pretty sure that's not how it works, Meg."

We accelerated through a fresh red light.

"If we're late, we're late," I said. "I want to arrive alive."

"Well, then you'd better stop commenting on my driving." With her left hand on the steering wheel, Mary contorted herself and attempted to reach her right hand into the back seat.

"Whatever it is, I can get it," I said.

"I need my 'B,'" Mary said. "It's somewhere back there."

I reached behind me and retrieved the sheet of paper, on which was printed a fancy sexy letter "B" topped with a crown tilted to the left.

"It looks a little bit like the Budweiser logo, doesn't it?" I said.

"Don't you even go there, Meg!" Mary said. "The 'B' is more elegant, and the crown is different."

"I guess it's more of a tiara," I said. A peace offering.

"Yeah, it's more girly, more of a 'queen' crown than a 'king.'"

After getting lost and circling the neighborhood in search of a parking space, we were properly thirty minutes late—which actually wasn't that bad by Mary's standards. The artist, Billy, a friend of a friend from Mary's work, looked like a grizzled Hell's Angel. Swords hung on the wall in that tattoo parlor. Mary and I both briefly had a "come to Jesus" moment.

Contrary to his appearance, though, Bill proved to be gentle, soft spoken, and magnanimous about the delay. Within a couple of minutes, we were talking about designs. Mary showed him her idea for the "B."

"What does it stand for?" Billy asked.

"Oh," Mary said. "'Blocher,' which is my last name."

"Okay," Billy said.

"But it's not just for Blocher," Mary added. "Think about it. 'Queen B,' like Beyoncé. Also 'B,' as in 'bi-yatch.' There are a lot of ways to interpret it!"

Next, Billy asked for my design. I produced the "wings" example I'd brought and explained the symbolism. I couldn't talk of Katie's passing without tearing up.

Mary and I both noticed that Billy seemed to be taking an extra-long time to prepare the images. Granted, two illustrations were not nothing, but how long could reproducing a crowned "B" and a pair of wings take?

Billy returned with the decals that would be permanently embossed onto our bodies. The "B," Mary happily observed, looked exactly like the one she had given him. The wings, though, which had been so modest in the print-out I had given him, were now massive, Eagles wings.

I made an "O" face.

"I needed to make it bigger in order to render the detail properly," Billy explained softly. "Otherwise it would just look dark. You wouldn't be able to see the feathers."

I was having serious second thoughts about going through with it. One, I was iffy on the idea in the first place; I didn't want to come out looking like Travis Barker or Dwayne "The Rock" Johnson. Two, the bigger and more intricate the tattoo, the more the pain—right?

"Go big or go home, Meg," Mary said.

I was a doe in the headlights, eyes aglow, frozen in place.

"She'll go first," Mary said.

In my head, I reviewed the situation. There was no way Mary was going to let me walk without getting the tattoo. To insist on going second would be to prolong the pain of anticipation. Watching Mary writhe under the sewing-machine-like needle would only make waiting harder, increasing my already acute fear.

"Sure," I heard myself saying. "I'll do it."

Billy directed me to get partially naked and lie down, right side up. I complied. He removed the backing from the decal, spread it carefully over my side, and pulled up the remaining sheet. It was "go" time.

Mary held my hand. As the needling began, what I experienced wasn't pain, exactly; I mean, I had given birth to two kids. The feeling was more like being scratched in slow-motion by a cat, or a million baby yellow jacket stings. After the initial shock, you get kind of used to the sensation, but then you start thinking, basically, "How long will this fucking take?"

Personally, I started bargaining with myself: "I can endure this if it only goes on for five more minutes." Mary held my hand, but her wincing facial expressions only served to amplify the "being poked repeatedly in the same place by a jagger bush" pain. I went as long as I could, then got ready to call it; I mean, I couldn't even bring myself to look to see what the progress was.

"Can I just have a minute?" I said.

"Oh, Meg," Mary said. "You don't have the experience of getting your hair done. That's like an all-day thing. What's the worst you've had to go through? Getting a perm?"

"I did get those extensions, remember," I said through gritted teeth.

"Meg," Mary said. "That was a one-off. Imagine doing that, or worse, a couple of times a month for your whole damn life."

I shut up. In retrospect, I don't know how I managed to not cry.

When it was her turn, Mary appeared completely damn unfazed. Her "B" was smaller than my wings, but it was still a tattoo: the buzz-saw needle did the same stabbing, the same stamping into the skin. Through it all, Mary looked like she was getting a pedicure. It was as though watching me get my tattoo was harder for her than going through the experience herself.

When it was over, and our throbbing tattoo wounds were wrapped in what appeared to be Saran wrap, Mary paid and we thanked Billy, who had been a doll. We retreated to Applebee's for a well-earned dinner and half-price martinis. We were both sore—given the location of my "wings," it hurt for me to laugh, to breathe. Mary's plan was to "drink ourselves numb," but we were both moms, and nursing wounds, and it was an early night.

Over the next few days, we called each other often to compare notes. For a while, I had some extreme buyer's remorse: I wished intensely that I had taken the first, non-tattoo road. Oh, to go back and have regular, non-ink-stamped skin! The idea had been to get something that you could almost not notice, and there was no not noticing, every single time I took my damn shirt off, the foot-long pair of angel wings on my right rib cage. There was also the itchiness, as my body desperately, and in vain, tried to "fight" the invading black ink.

"What did we do, Mary?" I said in our daily call.

"We did what we said we were going to do, Meg," Mary said. "You have a beautiful tribute to Katie, and I have my 'B.'"

"Mary, even with the lotion, my tattoo is so itchy. I know I'm not supposed to scratch it, so I'm trying to massage it with the top of my fingernail."

"That's scratching, Meg!"

"It's more of a graze."

Through the phone line: the cackle. "Meg, real talk, my 'B' is fine. There's just a tiny little itch in the crown area, and I'm not even using the Aquaphor you got. It's in your head, bestie. Be strong!"

Before long, Mary's tune had changed: "Meg, oh my god, this fucking 'B.' I'm gonna chew off my leg, it's so damn itchy. Can I borrow the Aquaphor? I can stop by on the way to work! Can you put it in your mailbox?"

In the deep recesses of my mind, I could hear Katie laughing at us, and maybe at our tattoos. But there was no way of going back and taking the other, un-inked road.

Mary never questioned her "B." In time, I came to love my wings as a constant reminder of Katie and a reflection of the permanent imprint her spirit, and her passing, left on my life.

The tattoo is also a tribute, of sorts, to Mary, and one of the many roads I traveled with my best friend — so many of which I wouldn't have dreamed of traversing without the courage and spirit of adventure she brought to my life. I carry within me the strength I gained through our relationship, forged in the fires of trials, tribulation, and adventure. Truly, it has made all the difference.

3. THE WAKE-UP TRIP

Life is a lot like the hills around Pittsburgh. Sometimes you're up, and the sun is out, the sky is clear, and all around are rolling hills swathed in green. Other times, you're down in a deep, dark gully, where the air is dark and tepid, and the rotten-egg smell of methane is inescapable.

A few months before I lost my baby sister, Katie, I also lost my job when the Art Institute entered its death spiral. I did finally find a position at Triangle Tech, another post-secondary school, which had its offices on Pittsburgh's North Side. Pittsburgh may be the city of bridges, but the rivers have a way of cleaving the town into pieces. My domain has always been the South Hills, south of the Monongahela River. Homestead and South Side I can do, but anywhere across a bridge, especially Downtown or anything adjacent to it, is a no go. The fact was, though, that I needed a job, so I would have to grin and bear the byzantine commute: Deposit "Foxy," my decaying 2003 Hyundai, at a park and ride near home; take a bus to town; walk to the Cultural District; take a second bus to Perrysville Avenue in the rain, snow, sleet, etc. (this is Pittsburgh). Like my mom, who, even in her mid-seventies, rarely goes to bed before the witching hour, I'm a night owl, but that was no longer going to work. Most mornings, my shift would start at 7:30 a.m., which meant that I'd have to set my alarm for 4:15, which was as ridiculous as it sounds. (I love my students, but who in the world has a financial aid crisis before eight o'clock in the morning?)

I was constantly exhausted. I had always been given to spacing out. Around this time, though, I'd actually nod off in the middle of conversation when Mary and I were out. Mary became fixated on the idea that I had narcolepsy.

"This is alarming," Mary would say. "What if you pass out when you're driving to the park-n-ride?"

"Mare," I'd say. "The park-n-ride is less than five minutes from my house!"

"A sudden attack of sleep can come at any time!"

Mary decided that I needed to reset and reboot. As usual, her solution was for us to go on a trip. Our friend Sara Strenk, who worked for a while with Mary as a property manager, lived near Baltimore and had suggested we come to visit. We could go to dinner, shop, get massages, and Sara would show us around town. The only problem was that every single one of those things, except maybe being shown around town, cost money, which neither Mary nor I had. We could (and sometimes did) have two dollars left and Mary would still insist: "Meg, we got this. We'll find a cheap flight and figure it out!" Of course, I knew we didn't have this, but I needed a damn break and was in no position to argue.

We arrived at the airport only to find that the airline was charging extra for every piece of checked baggage. While I get that companies need to make money, this practice unfairly discriminates against women and people with children, who tend to pack more heavily. By the time we each finished checking our bags, we had spent half of our "fun" money—no exaggeration. It was ludicrous.

We made it to Baltimore and, of course, it was wonderful to see Sara. By day two, though, we were wondering about quick fundraisers we could use to finance the rest of the trip. If further meals would be necessary, maybe we could work as maids at the hotel. Mary, Sara, and I all chipped in to make it work.

The next night was a planned outing at a really cool spot with a view of Baltimore. Mary and I both loved heels—I'm not tall, and Mary was flat-out short—and our shoes weren't cut out for the brick and cobblestone roads around the city. Our feet kept getting stuck in cracks and grooves in the streets; we were teetering like wounded Thompson's gazelles about to be finished off by cheetahs in the bush, not the vacationing models we'd hoped to be. It wasn't cheetahs that were stalking me, however, but sleep.

We were at this beautiful restaurant. Mary and Sara were laughing and having a good time, but I was becoming increasingly aware of the pull of gravity on all parts of my body. The next thing I felt was Mary shaking the shit out of me: "MEG, OH MY GOD, YOU ARE FALLING ASLEEP AT A RESTAURANT; WHAT THE FUCK?"

I was dreaming about work, where I was doing my millionth FAFSA application at 7:15 in the morning. It wasn't an especially good dream, but sleep is like good vanilla ice cream: Once you have a taste, you need more of it.

"MEG, I'M ALARMED. YOU NEED A DOCTOR IMMEDIATELY! THIS CAN'T BE RIGHT! IT'S NINE O'CLOCK, MEG!"

Once I was awake, I was good to go for the rest of the evening. We did shots, stopped for cheap pizza slices on the way back to the car, and laughed and laughed. We even got to visit with Mary's nephew, Christian.

When we got back to Pittsburgh, the causes of my emotional gully were still present but I was better able to handle them for a while. I am pleased to report that I didn't fall asleep and crash my car en route to the park-n-ride.

And, as it does, time passed.

A few months later, I found a position at All-State Career School, minutes from my house. My colleagues there were so sweet and supportive that the place soon became the work "home" I'd always been looking for. For this, I remain grateful.

It doesn't just take a village to raise a child; it takes a village to care for each and every one of us, regardless of our age. The more people, the better, but every single person helps in their own way.

3. THE WITCH AND THE BIG, BAD WOLF

Even a year after I lost my sister Katie, life was an everyday struggle. Part of the problem with such a loss is its permanence. No matter what you do—from beautiful moments of remembrance to trying to hear some kind of word from heaven to going to see a damn medium—the person you have lost is still beyond reach. The one coping mechanism that worked for me was theater. For actors, theater is life, and I needed life so badly to salve the pain. Katie had always been one of my biggest fans; I could hear her voice within me telling me to keep auditioning, keep using the degree I worked so hard for, keep creating and living.

Mary had gotten word through the Pittsburgh community theater grapevine that The Heritage Players were holding auditions for Stephen Sondheim's *Into the Woods.* Mary had already been in a Heritage Players production, loved Sondheim, and *Into the Woods* was one of her all-time favorite plays. The role of the Witch had been on Mary's theater bucket list for as long as I'd known her.

My feelings about *Into the Woods* were more mixed. In high school, I had played Cinderella's stepmother in a production put on by an organization called the Christian Drama Workshop (the "Christian" part arose from the theater's location in a church basement). Though I loved the role—I have affinities for darker characters and comedy—the show was really tough. Sondheim's music is beautiful, but it can be challenging (think four-part harmonies), and his shows are nearly all song. Singing is an outlet for me, but I consider myself an actress first and a singer second.

"Mare, this is a win, win, win!" I gushed on the phone.

"I don't know, Meg," Mary said. "This might have to be a pass for me."

"A pass?" I scoffed. "Why?"

"I'm at my limit helping Karen," Mary said. "Plus, did you see? They want us to audition with a monologue. I'm not trying to memorize a damn monologue right now."

"But it's The Heritage Players," I pleaded. "It's a chance to be the Witch! You've been preparing all your life!"

"Very funny, Meg," Mary said. "Schedule an audition time for yourself, and then I'll do it when I feel more on top of things."

Clearly, Mary was trying to politely back out, but I couldn't take "no" for an answer. Once again, it was our own, bestie version of "unstoppable force versus an immovable object." I took to pestering Mary via text, and even went as far as to send an email to schedule Mary an audition without her consent. I had to fight to get her there; I suspect Mary finally went along, monologue and all, for the good of our friendship.

In theater you have good auditions, bombs where everything's just off, and so-so ones. This time I really went in with confidence, gave it my all, and felt like fellow redhead Bernadette Peters. Mare was also up about her audition.

In any show, there are only so many roles that are right for actors in each age range. Though I was old for the Baker's Wife, I loved how quirky she was and had ideas for how to put my own comic spin on the character. Mary, of course, had set her sights on the Witch, and that was fine with me—it was, after all, her dream role.

I was thrilled to get a callback, but surprised by the role for which I was to audition: the Witch. I texted Mary tentatively: "Uh, Mare, they want me to audition for . . . the Witch."

Mary wrote back instantly: "Me, too!"

I was horrified. As actors and singers, Mary and I had different strengths. Though we both had comic chops, Mary had the thousand-watt voice. My strength was in bringing the idiosyncrasies out of a character. Never, in our years of auditions, had we been called back for the same part.

"We got this!" Mary texted after some delay, adding the women with bunny ears dancing emoji for a light touch.

Carried by this mutual bonhomie, Mary and I became Team Witch. Cue the montage of each of us, and both of us, visibly slaughtering "The Last Midnight" at first, then us sipping moscato, then us helping each other learn the scene, then us sipping moscato, then us seeming to nail, based on exaggerated, pumped fists, "The Last Midnight," then us sipping Moscato, then us having the scene down pat, then us doing a Moscato toast.

We met at the theater. Interest in this show had been huge and the callback hall was full. The mood was tense, our own tension heightened by the fact that Mary and I didn't know who we would be going up against. This we knew for sure: One of us damn well better get the part. If some third-party rando walked away with the role, it would be more than just a loss for both of us—it would be cruel, perverse judgment against our years of combined, often shared, experience, hard work, and (honorary) sisterhood.

At long last, the director announced the call for the Witch. Mary and I entered the room, looking wearily for the competition. We waited . . . and we waited. Finally, the terrible realization dawned on us: We would be competing head to head against each other.

With our dear friend Marian Bollman on piano, we ran through "The Last Midnight" one last time, together, like some version of Nora Dunn and Jan Hooks's "Sweeney Sisters" sketch.

Next we would have to sing for the room in front of each other. I went first. My rendition was all about timing and bringing out the comedy in the lines. By then, I was really vibing with my interpretation of the part, and, when I was finished, I was pleased with my performance.

Mary went next. She took more of a powerhouse approach to the song along the lines of Patina Miller or Phylicia Rashad, and she tore the roof off the damn place.

Nick, the director, asked us both whether, if we weren't cast, we would take a smaller role. Mary was a hard no. Ever the diplomat, I said I really wanted to work with Mary and my friend Steve Gallagher, who would play the Big Bad Wolf; only after the fact did it occur to me that I may just have sealed my own fate.

We decamped to Atria's, a slightly upscale restaurant in Pleasant Hills, and made nervous conversation as we ordered our five-dollar martinis. Whatever the outcome, we had to toast to the unique obstacle we had faced and overcome together, with love—the same way we'd made it over the countless hurdles that had come before.

Before we had finished the first round, Mary's phone rang. Time slowed down and the look of rapture on Mary's face told the story. She had landed the Witch. When my phone rang, all that remained was formality. Once again, I would perform the role of Cinderella's stepmother. Though there was some slight disappointment on my part, I was legitimately thrilled for Mary's opportunity to put her stamp on the role of her dreams.

I'd like to be able to say that the Witch audition was the only point of controversy between Mary and me in this show. Alas, there was also the significant matter of the Big Bad Wolf, Steve Gallagher.

Steve and I originally met in a play called "Over the Tavern." In back-to-back productions in different theaters, we played the married couple Ellen and Chet Pazinski, coheads of a working-class Polish family struggling with questions around faith in Buffalo in 1959. Our onstage vibe was very much Alice and Ralph Kramden. Steve was perfectly suited for his role: of Irish descent, with dark hair and eyes, he looked like a cross between Jackie Gleason and a mob boss.

Our working relationship soon evolved into a friendship. When, a few short months later, I lost my sister, Katie, it was Steve, along with therapy and antidepressants, and of course Mary, that kept me going. Similar to Mary, Steve was loud and sarcastic but also had a sweet, caring side that came through in his relationship with his son. His humor and sensitivity lifted me up, carrying me through the day-to-day struggle of living with grief.

Mary had always been fiercely protective of me and our friendship. She saw Steve as a threat, not only to her friendship with me, but to me personally; she was worried that he wouldn't respect boundaries and wreak havoc on my life. Steve, for his part, couldn't really get what Mary's problem was, and he wasn't the kind of person to back down or shy away from conflict. Mary and Steve were both cordial and professional, but I could feel the underlying tension whenever the three of us were in a room together—which, as we were all part of the "Into the Woods" cast, was often.

Mary and Steve had great respect for each other's talents, but, aside from that, they were just very different people. Mary was born to be a "rogue." Steve was less than charmed by Mary's pathological lateness, which he saw as selfish.

"I don't care if she stays late," Steve said one day as we waited for Mary. "Arriving late, though, is just rude."

I sighed. "It's just who Mary is. It's not personal. I've known Mare for more than twenty years, and she's always been like this."

"It doesn't matter whether the intent is personal," Steve said. "You have to look at the *effect on others*. Mary's lateness personally affects Nick, you, me, the whole cast. Rehearsal goes long because it starts late. People have partners, families, work the next day. It's shitty."

The next shoe dropped when, as we were moving into the critical rehearsal stage, Mary dyed her hair neon red. Nick, the director, was not thrilled because now the only option would be for her to wear a wig. Actors routinely wear wigs in productions, but it was another thing to worry about.

"I asked him prior to if I could go red," Mary said on the ride home from rehearsal. "He approved it. Where's the issue?"

"Did you say what color red you were going to dye it?" I asked.

"I just said, 'red,'" Mary said. "And it *is* red. I asked Nick! I said, 'What shade of red would you have been okay with?' And do you know what he said?"

In fact, I was afraid to hear what Nick said.

"He said, 'A color found in nature.'" Mary sucked her teeth. "The jagoff."

Steve, of course, was on team Nick, and he was not the kind of person to hide his feelings. Though he wasn't afraid to confront Mary, or anyone, his preferred approach was to layer on the sarcasm. Mary, of course, would give it right back to him. Things were getting uncomfortable.

"You're pissed about the hair," I said to Steve on the phone. "Look, I get it."

"Just another selfish decision," Steve said. "Mary only thinks about Mary."

"She's been going through a lot," I said. This was true. Mary's beloved sister, Karen, had been struggling with diabetes-related issues. Her marriage with Ryan, always mercurial, had recently been more off than on, though both parties were trying to work through their issues for the good of their family.

"Life is hard," Steve said. "But a commitment is a commitment."

"She's stubborn and set in her ways," I said. "It's part of her essence, her magic. It's Mare being Mare."

"At what point does 'Mare being Mare' become a copout?" Steve said.

I needed to put things into perspective for him.

"Steve," I said. "Mary is my best friend. She has been with me every step of the damn way in life. You name it, she has been there—and she's been there one hundred percent. You don't want to get me started listing all the specifics because, I swear to God, once I start I won't be able to stop."

"Meg," Steve said. "I believe you. Personally, though, I haven't seen any of that. She hasn't been with *us* every step of the way. It's like she's doing us a favor, being in the show, which is bullshit. When you get one of the major roles in a production, it's a privilege."

"Maybe you should talk to Mare," I said.

"How do you think that would go, Meg?"

Steve had a point.

"Look," I said. "This whole thing has gotten really awkward for me. I love Mary, you are also one of my best friends, and I have so much respect and appreciation for Nick."

"I'll do the best I can," Steve said. "But it's a two-way street. If Mary sends anything my way, I'm going to give it back to her in kind."

"Fair enough," I said. "Thank you."

"You got it, friend," Steve said. "I will try."

On the way to practice, I gently raised the issue with Mary: "I think they just feel a way about the lateness," I said. "And the hair."

"This is who I am," Mary said. "They know I'm gonna be who I am. The way they're treating me is disrespectful. They don't know what I'm dealing with. They don't know that I lost both of my parents. They don't know about Karen being sick. They don't know about Ryan being Ryan."

"Maybe if you said something about those things," I said, "they'd understand more."

"That's a 'no,'" Mary said. "I'm not just going to, like, up and open up about my life, my challenges, in front of them. If they cared, they'd ask."

"I don't think that's how most people operate," I said. "Even if they do care. And Steve and Nick definitely care."

Mary sucked her teeth. This was something she only did when a situation had crossed over into "fucked up beyond any repair" territory.

"Steve can be sarcastic," I said. "He can be blunt. But what he's really trying to do is protect. He's protecting me. He's protecting himself. He's protecting the show."

Mary drove on in silence. We were only about five minutes away from rehearsal; I wished it were twenty. Hell, I wished we weren't even going to rehearsal. I needed a damn break.

"You don't have to talk to Steve," I said. "I mean, beyond pleasantries."

"I'm not sharing pleasantries with that piece of work," Mary said. "Or with Nick."

More silence.

"Can you at least keep things civil?" I said. "For me?"

"I love you, Meg," Mary said. "I don't know why some of your friends are your friends, but you are my bestie. I'll do the best I can."

After a Saturday show, the cast gathered at a bar. I was getting over an untimely viral infection. I was sitting at a long table with Mary on one side and Steve on the other, doing the "Switzerland" thing, trying to keep everyone happy. I was struggling to be heard over the booming music, and dividing my attention between two of my best friends was exhausting.

Finally, Mary rose to go smoke outside. When I turned to Steve, I was alarmed to see that he was getting up, too. My first instinct was to run after them, but something—trust?—held me back. They were both adults. They were both brilliant and kind. They could figure it out.

Three minutes passed. Five. At the ten-minute mark, overcome by a combination of morbid curiosity and fear, I hurried outside. Mary and Steve were both sharp as hell, with great "word venom." Would the Witch be skinning the Big Bad Wolf? Would the Wolf be pulling the Witch down into a tar pit? The last thing I wanted was to wind up as collateral damage, black mascara tears rolling down my face as the uncaring, suburban Pittsburgh traffic scrolled past.

To my surprise, I found myself interrupting what seemed to be a regular, light-hearted conversation between Mary and Steve about none other than . . . me. (No shortage of material there, right?)

"Just came out to check," I said sheepishly.

"The woman herself!" Steve said. Translation: "We're talking about you."

"We're good, Meg," Mary said. Translation: "Go away, please."

I was touched. Two of my best friends were finding common ground and attempting to be cool . . . for me. Two of the strongest, most talented, most stubborn people I knew were working to bury the hatchet and overcome their differences . . . for me. If that meant they had to talk a little smack about their common friend, so be it; I was happy to let my foibles fuel the warming flames of détente. The resulting warmth would not only save me a lot of grief but strengthen our work on stage.

Relieved, I left the Witch and the Big Bad Wolf out there on the sidewalk and went back inside to join the rest of the cast. As I walked, the theme song from "Into the Woods," played through my mind: "Into the woods, who knows what may be lurking on the journey? Into the woods, to get the thing that makes it worth the journeying!"

Theater was always a passion for Mary and me, and it saved us more than once. But the "thing that makes it worth the journeying" wasn't the glow of the lights, or the roar of the crowd, or even the artistry that went into imbuing a character with life and soul. No, what made the journey worthwhile was camaraderie, love, and moments like the one out on the sidewalk, when two diametrically opposed people chose to follow the pebbles of goodwill toward understanding and friendship.

4. TAKE ME TO HEAVEN

I have come to dread early morning phone calls from friends and loved ones. On the beautiful spring morning of Tuesday, May 8, 2018, I was getting myself and the kids ready when Ryan called. Karen, Mary's sister, had died. The representative from the personal care home who called Mary had said, straight up, "Karen has unfortunately expired." She was fifty-six.

Karen, or "KJ" as we called her, first appeared on my radar when Mary and I were at Point Park. She was there with Mary and her parents for first-year orientation and move-in day. Karen was like an extension of Mary; I could tell even from a distance, based on the way their big personalities and huge laughs played off each other, that Mary and Karen were tight.

Because they were born fourteen years apart, Karen was, if anything, more second mother than sister or friend to Mary. Even with the age difference, they had much in common: Karen and Mary were both raised around the church, both loved gospel music, and, in the secular realm, both were quick-witted. You always wanted to be the person listening to Karen and Mary being funny; you never wanted to be the person at whom their razor-sharp, frequently hilarious broadsides were aimed. Karen was unlucky in love, and Mary was fiercely protective of her older sister. Nobody was good enough for Karen.

Karen had also been something of a role model for Mary. She was smart and had a long career as a manager at PNC Bank locations around Western Pennsylvania. She was deeply visual and showed this both through the way she dressed herself and the wreaths and floral arrangements she crafted by hand. Years before Airbnb and VRBO, Karen's house looked like an ad. It also served as somewhat of a getaway for Mary when she was younger. Though Karen was every bit as pious as her parents, she loved Mary way too much to ever give up her secrets.

Another early memory I have of Karen was in the Swinburne Street era. My parents had given me the little blue Christmas tree that used to stand on a table in our living room. Karen, who loved Christmas, helped us put the tree up both years we lived in our apartment and made tiny paper angels and silver bows to serve as ornaments. Mary and I reciprocated by inviting Karen to our parties. Karen was older than us and decidedly not the party type, but, when she could, she assisted with setup or cleanup, or brought over some of her famous homemade pepperoni rolls—like the second mom to Mary that she was.

In the post-college years, Mary was a fixture at shared family functions, showers and Christenings, and anything involving fancy decorations or meticulously arranged spreads of finger food. This was Karen's domain. Mary and I started a tradition of taking Karen and Jenny, both fall babies, to P. F. Chang's for their birthdays. Between Karen and Mary, either of whom could have been a comedian in a parallel life, the laughs far outlasted the fancy cocktails.

Like Mr. J and Mary, Karen was diabetic. I never really put it all together because Karen wasn't the kind of person to talk about her struggles. Also, diabetes does its damage in eerie silence. The whole idea of the body losing its ability to "unlock" blood sugar and turn it into energy feels abstract. Without treatment, though, the lingering, unprocessed glucose can attack the cardiovascular system, the nerves, the kidneys, and the eyes. Diabetes also compounds: The body is always working, trying to break down the blood sugar; after a certain point, its mechanisms for processing glucose start to fail, which has a cascading effect.

Around 2014, Karen started having problems with her vision—the first domino to fall. Frequent, painful injections were required. It was only the beginning; Karen's health declined rapidly from there, and she was in and out of the hospital until her death.

Mary became a "prayer warrior" for her sister and reached out to her network repeatedly for prayers and positive vibes in search of a miracle. But Mary also worked small miracles herself. One hospital visit, Mary brought Karen a new wig. Karen and Mary were both such visual people, and hair was extremely important to both of them. Mary knew that Karen's hair was a disaster from all the time spent in bed coupled with no salon time. It was a light moment watching Mary beautify her sister, then saying, "Next, Kare, Jesus, we gotta wax that lip!" Karen laughed so hard. Of course, the wig looked phenomenal, and the new look gave Karen a boost.

After that hospital visit, with Karen's vision worsening, it didn't seem like a good idea for her to live at home. Karen began to suffer swelling in her lower extremities, which, in time, became so bad that she was basically confined to bed. In her fifties, Karen was easily one of the youngest people in the personal care home. On her best days, she still radiated her trademark verve. The nursing assistants all loved her for her generosity of spirit and humor, even in the face of distressingly worsening symptoms.

One of the last lead roles Mary played was Delores in *Sister Act* at the Grand Theater in Elizabeth; this was another one of our shared productions, with me cast as crazy sister Mary Patrick (a little too on the nose?). Karen would typically never miss a chance to see Mary perform, and she wanted badly to see her sister tearing the roof off singing "Fabulous Baby" in this show.

Mary worked hard to arrange for Karen to get an Access paratransit ride to the show. Just before the Sunday matinee performance, Mary received a devastating call from Karen: Although she was all dolled up and ready, the van hadn't shown up. As it was just a few minutes before curtain, new arrangements couldn't be made. Mary, in her usual way, powered through, but I could see how much she was hurting. Karen was hurting, too.

At the care home, the nursing assistants tried to cheer her up, and when we talked to her later, Karen even laughed with us a little bit. Still, we all felt like we had missed an opportunity to bring some light into Karen's life. The disappointment and pain was still lingering a few days later when Mary got the terribly brutal call from the care home: "Karen has unfortunately expired."

Mary asked me to come. She needed me, so of course I was going. I called off work and made a beeline for Mary's house. When I got there, my best friend was still sobbing, beside herself with grief.

"Not my sister, Meg," Mary said. "My parents, then Katie, and now my sister! Why? Oh my God, why? When will this fucking end?"

I held Mary and tried to calm her. "Karen was in so much pain," I said. "She's in a better place now. If anyone's going to heaven, Karen is."

"I know, I know," Mary said. "But I want her to be here with me! Just for another minute, please! Oh God, how can I lose my parents and my sister?"

The question was legit. As I knew, Christianity has several answers, but they're all opaque: God works in mysterious ways; God knows what is right and best and we must accept what He decides. It doesn't feel good to question those answers, but what are you supposed to tell your friend when her sister has died alone at a personal care home at the age of fifty-six?

We made the short drive to see Karen. All around us, life was beginning anew. As bleak as Western Pennsylvania can be in the winter, it is positively Eden-like in the spring: The hills are all swathed in green; the flowers and cherry trees and dogwoods are in blossom; the robins, catbirds, and mockingbirds, returned for the warmer months, are busy feeding and assembling their nests. Spring is the time for rebirth and life, and yet, in the car, we were grappling with death.

When we got to the care home, we encountered a similar dichotomy. On the outside, the place was oddly serene, with fresh paint and carefully tended gardens; inside, though, the air was cold and stale, each room bisected and trisected by partitions. The maze-like layout of the home was reminiscent of Cedars Sinai, albeit on a smaller scale: Once again, I felt like I was being pulled in quicksand down endless corridors into a nightmare. Mary and I clung to each other, sobbing, afraid to open our eyes completely. When we rounded the corner into Karen's room, Mary threw herself on Karen, screaming and crying, and I, in turn, collapsed onto both of them. There were, and are, no words.

Mary used up every dime in her 401K and exhausted all her resources to plan a beautiful wake and ceremony for Karen. Because she didn't feel capable of singing at the funeral, she recorded herself in advance.

That day—and every day—the song "Take Me to Heaven" from "Sister Act" echoes through my head: " . . . when you strut your stuff / And you do your thing / I just can't help surrendering / You're so strong, you're so sweet / You're what makes me complete." Though the song is obviously about God, I hear the lyrics as an ode to sisters, biological and otherwise. I can see Karen and my sister Katie dressed to the nines, even when it wasn't necessary, doing their "thing." And I can see the way sisters, biological or otherwise, make each other's lives complete:

Elevating, transfiguring the day-to-day grind into something more meaningful, and also more manageable, not to mention more colorful and fun.

Mary and I both lost sisters. Both names started with *K-a.* Both women were unique, larger than life, and way, way too young to go. Mary and I were both crushed beyond words, but she had me and I had her—not off in the distance, not in "thoughts and prayers" or flowers and a card. When our hearts were breaking, we were there at each other's side, broken heart next to broken heart, soul next to soul. In this soulmate light, we could repair, restore, and begin to heal. You don't get over the loss of a sister, but a sister, a best friend, someone who gets you as you get them, can help guide you through the hardest days, hours, weeks, years . . .

Karen, we will always miss you, love you. Your light shines on in my heart.

5. POINT OF NO RETURN

With money being continually tight, the trips to Myrtle Beach were not going to be an every-year occurrence. Steve and I tried to think of someplace within easy driving range of Pittsburgh that would still feel like a vacation, and we settled on the Splash Lagoon Indoor Water Park Resort in Erie, Pennsylvania. Though it wasn't the beach, there would be plenty for the kids to do. For some reason, we found ourselves with a little extra money, so we decided to rent a suite on the ground floor and invite the Blochers.

Though we all had fun, the vibe was just slightly off, as though a figure lurking offstage had put a hex on the trip. We were only there for two days and three nights. Max, who felt that a true vacation should be a whole week, had a meltdown on day two. We were still very much in the process of trying to navigate Max's meds at the time, and we totally got stuck in a loop where no one could calm Max down—though in retrospect, he had a point: Splash Lagoon < Myrtle Beach.

For her part, Michaela was in that stage where she wasn't always feeling people; true blue Virgo that she was, she projected a strident self-assuredness and would get sarcastic and brooding; think of the titular character of the "Beavis and Butthead" spinoff "Daria" if her needs weren't met. Once again, in retrospect: Understood. Kayla was fifteen, trapped in the solipsistic amber of her age.

Several hours into our trip, Kayla wasn't feeling swimming pools, water slides, or otherwise being doused with water. She wanted to return to the room and be a teenager. Uncle Ryan, likewise, wasn't feeling the vibe, so he offered to go back with his niece. There was plenty of room in the suite for those two to do their things, whatever they were.

I'll be the first person to admit that adulthood and adult relationships can both be hard. When we're young, we all have dreams, ideas of what we can become. How well-defined the dreams are varies from person to person, but we all have some kind of vision for how things will be. And some of us, no doubt, realize something like that vision. Many of us, though, find ourselves working five days a week in a job that maybe isn't our dream job, at best, or is really hard, at worst. This isn't a complaint; it's just a statement of fact.

Even the best jobs take a toll, but the tradeoff feels fair. When your job is harder, less of a fit for you as a person, you wake up every day feeling defeated. And there are so many ways for a job to be hard: They can be physically demanding, psychologically tough, low paying, or they can be basically fine but something other than what we had in mind for ourselves. Of course, some people have to suffer through jobs that check all of those boxes.

Now, into this mix, add a spouse who is also working and facing similar challenges, and kids whose needs change radically over time but never really decrease, even under the best of circumstances. It's easy to see how the family dream—happy parents, thriving kids—can be hard to realize. Few people ever live in that happy, idealized place. For many of us, life is a grind, and over time, it can take a toll on each of us personally.

In an ideal world, we'd all have access to the kind of mental health support—friends, church, theater, recreational sports, a loving, extended family, therapy, Zumba, antidepressants, you name it—to get us through the hard times and keep us growing. No doubt, many people take advantage of one or several of those things and find their own way of thriving. For a variety of reasons, others can't, or don't. What happens when life is hard over time and our mental, physical, or spiritual needs aren't met is that our struggles metastasize. We're all so connected; it's inevitable that, when a person is feeling pain, they spread some of the hurt into their relationships, where it compounds.

Things between Steve and me had gotten more complicated over time. At root, Steve and I were friends first. Steve has an element that is calming to me, and, for my part, I can bring him out of himself and into the world. We married relatively young by today's standards, and we were very much in love. As with most couples, though, we didn't have a clue about what kinds of challenges lay down the road for us. Money was often tight. We didn't see much of each other during the week, and by the evenings and weekends, we had little energy to devote to our relationship. Our children are both brilliant, but all kids have challenges—and the hurdles that lay ahead for Max in particular were daunting, not only for him but for his parents and sister. And then my sister died.

We all deal with adversity in different ways, and I am not perfect. I lead with my heart, so while compassion comes naturally, I'm also sensitive, which can manifest in different ways depending on the situation. As an actor, I thrive on affirmation, and that has driven me to social media. Some people feel I post too much, or that my posts are too personal, or passive-aggressive, but the truth is that I post as much as I feel like I need each day to get by.

Where I feel openly, Steve often buries the hard things within, which can take the form of depression and hiding. After our family got a cat, Lyra, Steve claimed that his allergies were out of control and began to spend more and more time in our basement, his "man cave," where Lyra had never trod. This also conveniently removed Steve from everything going on upstairs, especially with Max. This shift made me feel unsupported, unwanted, and lonely. People told me that I was being dramatic, and, sure, I'm an actor, but the truth is that you can't have a healthy partnership, much less a relationship—much less a family—when one partner is in the basement 90 percent of the time.

I understand that, for Steve, his "man cave" is a coping mechanism. I will always love Steve, and that love, and the concentric circles of care and support surrounding it—our family, Steve's family, my family—keep us together. Steve has been my husband for almost twenty-five years. I don't expect or need the honeymoon days of the late nineties, but things have been hard for a while, and we both need to do some work.

Something I've learned in life is not to assume that I have it worse than the people around me. I knew that Mary and Ryan had had their issues, but I was about to learn that they were struggling far more than Steve and me.

From the beginning, Mary and Ryan had been "different." When I introduced them, the effect was instantaneous, like mixing vinegar with baking soda. There was an electricity between them that I sometimes envied. Ryan fawned after Mary, and Mary opened her heart to Ryan. They were madly in love, and they were happy for a long time.

One similarity to my relationship with Steve was that Mary was the "star," and Ryan was totally happy to hang back. A difference was that Ryan was quieter than Steve, more reserved, less comfortable in social situations, which led to him being a homebody (which Mary could never be). Family was always important to Ryan. He desperately wanted to be a dad. When he and Mary had Kennedy and Daunte, it was as though the finishing touches had been added to his identity: He was complete. Ryan, Kennedy, and Daunte were regulars at area playgrounds, climbing gyms, and arcades. Everyone commented on what a great, natural dad Ryan was.

Back when he had hair, Ryan was a redhead, and he was sensitive like I am. Sometimes the dam would burst. I remember back when Steve and I were planning our wedding, I had wanted to keep things small, and I wasn't sure whether we could invite Jeremy, a key childhood friend of Steve and Ryan's. They had all grown up in challenging circumstances in Heritage Hills, a lower income rental development not far from my parents' house. I loved Jeremy—anyone who has met Jeremy and knows his essence loves him—but I'm from a big, Catholic family and the number of invitees kept going up and up. I was also concerned that Jeremy wouldn't be able to afford a tux.

At some point, Ryan snapped and started sobbing. He stood up and gave the most impassioned speech I'd ever heard a man give about his friends: "We grew up protecting each other: Me, Steve, Harry, and Chris. We were the main crew at Heritage Hills. We were brothers, ride or die, and we are always going to be brothers. It wouldn't be right to leave Jeremy out and I won't fuckin' do it." Jeremy was in. Steve and Ryan split the cost of his tux. Steve was late to our wedding rehearsal, picking Jeremy up.

Mary and Ryan had loved with a kind of fearless abandon, and maybe that was why the hard times were so spectacularly hard. Even in better days, on the Myrtle Beach trips, Mare and Ry would usually have one big blowout fight at some point. In fairness to them, in a weird way, vacations can be stressful for everyone involved. Still, it was hard for Steve and me to see our friends go at it so viciously, and it was uncomfortable for both sets of kids.

So there we were on our first day at Splash Lagoon. Michaela and Ryan had gone to the suite ahead of us. Kayla was doing her thing in her room; fair enough. Ryan, though, had foregone the nap and, instead, polished off much of the case of beer he and Steve had purchased for the weekend. This was unlike the Ryan that Steve and I knew. As with many younger couples, we drank casually together. There had been some hints that Ryan had started drinking more heavily, but because it wasn't right out in front of us, we could look the other way. We couldn't do that in a shared suite. For her part, Mary was embarrassed, but also resigned: "This is what he does." It wasn't a new situation for her.

That night we had our official "game night": board games and cards with our best friends. We were playing Balderdash, having fun. Ryan was, if not on top of his proverbial game, managing to hold it together. In the other room—for once on vacation, we had plenty of room in which to stretch out—the kids, tired from a day of swimming and splashing, were starting to bicker. We tried to ignore them, but then it got heated and Kennedy screamed, "Daunte, owww!"

Somewhere inside Ryan's head, the gumband snapped. In a blind rage, he ran into the room and started going off on his kids. He was always a big, burly guy, but without the warmth that had been as much of a part of Ryan as his twinkling eyes, the vibe was more menacing. Things just imploded from there. Kennedy began to cry, and that triggered Mary; what had begun as a tired-kids spat between siblings morphed, in an instant, into a full-on verbal spat between Mary and Ryan, worse by several degrees of magnitude than we had seen on the Myrtle Beach trips. All the kids were upset; it was a mess.

When the storm had passed, everyone needed a little space. Mary claimed one of the decks and sat down. I followed her out.

Bejeweled with tears, Mary's brown eyes glistened in the night. Mary produced her cannabis vape pen and took a deep inhale to help her find her zen. For a while, we just let the sound of the summer night choir—crickets, cicadas, and katydids—salve our wounds.

Finally, Mary recrossed her legs, took a drag from her pen and exhaled. "I'm fucking *done*," she said, finally, to the night as much as me. "I can't do this anymore. I can be miserable all by myself. Two miserable people only make more misery for everyone. We're like damn Felisha and Deebo in 'Friday.'"

I thought about my own hard times with Steve. For us, there had always been the friendship to fall back on; it was almost like we were friends more than married partners, but at least there was that. I thought about the relationships I'd been around that were truly done, where people were just going through the motions, zombie-like, because that was what they felt they had to do. All couples have problems, issues, fights, but couples at the end of their ropes fight differently. Whereas a healthy argument can serve as an airing of grievances that gives way to a constructive conversation, a "done" fight is destructive, with each person slashing and burning, trying to inflict maximum emotional damage on the other and, through this, the relationship.

Mary and Ryan had tried saving the relationship: Things had been rough before they had Daunte, and the fact of handsome, charming, smart Daunte, had, for a while, righted the ship. Later they had gone to couples therapy, but, for that to be productive, you need some kind of healthy relationship material to work with. Mary loved the person Ryan had been, and Ryan still thought Mary was gorgeous. That wasn't enough, though, for them to save their relationship.

Divorce was hard financially, hard emotionally, and could do irreparable damage to innocent, developing children. On the other hand, toxic relationships, and the fights that resulted, could be at least as harmful to everyone involved. At some point, and I can't really blame Mary or Ryan, the air in their relationship had fouled, and now it was choking everyone unlucky enough to be in the room.

I would like to say that, out on the deck, I supported Mary's idea to forge her own, separate path, but it wasn't the way I had been raised. My parents had endured very tough times, and now they were, in their own weird way, soulmates.

"Mary," I heard myself saying. "Ryan loves you. You have two beautiful kids. You fight dirty because you are both stubborn and nobody backs down. He's using the beer to cope, just like you use your vape pen. Let things calm down and get back to normal."

"That's the thing," Mary said. "This shit *is* normal."

"Sleep on it. Maybe it's reversible."

"Reversible to what, Meg?" Mary said. "There's no going back. The damn ship has sunk. I'm in survival mode 24/7, and no one can keep that up. You get tired. You start to sink. I'm sinking, Meg, and I need to save myself."

It was hard to argue the point. The crickets and katydids and cicadas seemed to offer their blessing to the idea.

"I mean, damn," Mary said, and took another hit from her vape pen. "Here we are in beautiful Erie. The suite is nice, but let's call it what it is: Erie, Pennsylvania. Even with both of us married, we can't afford Myrtle Beach. Max was right: Vacation should be a damn week. But why would I want to be on vacation for a week with Ryan? Splash Lagoon, hell; we could be in damn Fiji and we'd both be miserable. You know it."

"Yes," I admitted, finally, to Mary and myself.

If, before, Mary and Ryan had been "figuring it out," from this point on their status would be more "separated." If, previously, there had been cracks, there was now a fissure, and it would only widen.

Mary and Ryan would still live together and coparent, and there would still be, in the formal sense, a marriage and a family, and there was still, unquestionably, love. Any hope for reconciliation, though, was irretrievably lost in time's murky abyss.

In the last years of her life, Mary became committed to finding a path out, and despite my own personal misgivings, I supported her one hundred percent.

Though Mary never stopped self-medicating, some of the fire definitely returned as she sought to forge a way forward for herself and her children. A symbolic step forward was the purchase of her treasured new, green Kia. Next she found a job at a great property management firm with a boss she loved. She was eyeing her own place in the near future.

I will never understand how relationships change the way they do. One thing I do know is that, if you aren't one of the two people in a marriage, you don't know all the facts. Or, as it says in the Bible, "Judge not, that ye be not judged." Live and let live. Love and let thrive. Sometimes the difference between struggling and thriving is having the courage to let go.

6. "WE ARE NOT OKAY"

My son Max's thirteenth birthday party was fast approaching. Mary was sick with bronchitis and had dropped off the radar. I had been trying to reach her for days. I'll never forget the long, recorded message she had for callers that ended with "Leave a message and I'll call you back . . . if you're not boring, that is." I left three long messages, then I couldn't leave any more because her voicemail was full. I texted her repeatedly. I even tried to reach her via Facebook Messenger. Radio silence on Mary's end.

Any time things went quiet between Mary and me, we would both take to social media. The posting of passive-aggressive quotes on Facebook was our shared weapon of choice. Things like, "The only way to have a friend is to be one," overlaid onto a background image of little girls hugging on the beach. Or "Never leave a friend behind" superimposed onto a picture of a fluffy kitten casting a forlorn gaze into the ether. BURN. I'm not proud.

After the passage of what I considered to be more than enough damn time, I would take one last stab at reaching out to Mary and leave the "communication" rubber ball in her court. The message was always some variation of, "Hey Mare, it's me. I'm worried, but I don't want to look like an ass here. Are you upset with me for something? If so, let's discuss. This is silly. I will leave it to you to reach back out. This is my last call. I love you." This would almost always lead to a return call from Mary that started icy and ended up fine, with us laughing for hours.

By the night before Max's party, I still hadn't heard anything from Mary. Max is like a (not so) little fish, so I had planned a hotel pool party at the Marriott on the Waterfront in Homestead for the last weekend in February. Mary's son, Daunte, was not only Max's best friend, but his only friend. The rest of the guest list comprised Michaela, Jenny, Jenny's son Colton, and Mary and Kennedy. Under normal circumstances, Mary and I would have planned the celebration together and spoken dozens of times on the phone, but she was icing my ass out. It was bad.

Once, when they ran into each other at Walgreens, Mary admitted to my sister Jenny that she knew I was sensitive, and when we were in disagreement, sometimes she left me hanging out there just to get a rise (insert evil, maniacal laugh).

That night, I had a dream, not about Mary, but my sister Katie. There wasn't anything super revelatory about the dream: Katie showed up at Max's party as though it were totally normal. We were all so glad to see Katie, to be able to hug her and tell her how much we missed her. The thing was, in the dream, we didn't even have to speak to be able to communicate. All we had to do was think and understand. This meant that our exchanges were pure and unclouded by the ambiguity of language. In the dream, what was exchanged was pure love.

Why was communication so damn hard? Most people are fortunate to have a big enough vocabulary, in theory, to be able to express what is on their minds. By the same token, most people on the other end are able to perceive and understand what has been said. What was the problem, then?

Part of the problem, yes, is that we sometimes don't choose the best words to convey our ideas. Also, for various reasons, we don't always say exactly what we mean, but instead talk in a kind of code. Complicating things, the listener doesn't receive the "code" in a vacuum, but through the lens of their own experience—or, like, whatever they happen to be going through in a given moment. Often, the speaker is zigging and the listener is zagging, and the intended meaning is lost somewhere between formulation and "decoding." Texting and social media only make this worse. Bad, nasty stuff ensues.

When we arrived at the hotel with Jenny and Colton, there had still been nothing, not even an emoji, from Mary. Though I wanted badly for the day to be about Max, I was distracted—and pissed off. What the heck had happened to my best damn friend? Moreover, what the heck had happened to our friendship? Mary and I had been besties for decades, and now she had randomly decided to ghost me before my son's party? I decided to play the "birthday boy" card: I had Max call Daunte's cell and check in. I listened closely as the conversation played out:

"Hi, Daunte, this is Max. Are you coming tonight? Oh good. I know you are always late. We didn't know for sure because Aunt Mare is being unresponsive and ignoring my mom."

"Oh My God, Max," I whispered under my breath. "Hang up!"

The first swim session came and went. What seemed like a long while later, Mary showed up with Daunte. I knew I had done nothing wrong, so unless she spoke to me first and explained what the hell was going on, it was going to be an awkward-ass night. From the jump, I could tell that there would be no such explanation from Mary, much less an apology. I opened the door to find an ice queen, as cold as un-gloved Elsa in *Frozen.* Mary was conspicuously without her Hello Kitty suitcase—so there would be no swimming or spending the night.

As Mary slinked through the door, she made no eye contact with me, which took some work with the two queen-sized beds, plus all the people and our stuff. I managed a low-energy "hey," and got the same from Mary. It was painful.

Mary made a beeline for Jenny, hugged her, and engaged in conversation as her normal, charming self. I could tell my sister felt completely awkward, caught in the middle. The boys were all oblivious and really couldn't care less; they just wanted to swim. I had ordered a few pizzas for the boys and a special chicken salad for Mary, Jenny and me. Mary barely touched the food.

We all took the boys down to the pool. As we sat poolside, Jenny between us, and watched the boys and Steve toss the football, I tried to strike up conversation.

"Colton can really throw that ball, Jen," I said.

"He's a football player, Meg," Jenny said.

The sound of splashes and boys playing echoed through the room. Mary offered nothing.

I decided to try a different tack. "Let's compare each of the boys to a shark," I said.

"What?" Jenny said.

"You know," I said. "Like, take Max. He's more of a floater than a swimmer. So let's call him a basking shark."

"I can't really think of any good sharks," Jenny said. "Hammerhead, great white, blue shark. None of those really fit anybody."

Once again, silence.

Finally, I broke down. I craned my neck to get a clear view of Mary. "So Mare, what the hell is up? I've been calling and not hearing back from you."

Mary responded with a performative, "Uh-huh," then turned to poor Jenny and started dishing: "Jen, I just found out we could all be getting laid off from my office. I've been extremely sick. It's been a total shit show. I need to get my drink on, like Crown Royal."

I cut in: "Do you want a wine spritzer, Mare? If you're worried about driving, you can still spend the night if you want."

Mary waited a beat for effect. "I'm good."

"Are you still feeling sick?" I said.

Another beat. "Not as bad as I was."

"That really sucks about your job," I said. "Are you definitely getting laid off?"

An especially long pause. "I don't know."

"You know I went through the same thing," I said.

Ten, fifteen seconds passed. "Yes," Mary said.

It was brutal.

Finally, Mary rose and said she needed to go home. She accepted our offer to drive Daunte home the next day—and I had to give her credit for not dragging her wonderful son into the conflict. Back in the room, she collected her coat, and agreed to take some of the salad I'd ordered for her, a goodie bag, and a huge slice of cake.

"Bye," she said dryly as she left. "Thanks for the food!"

The burn lingered long after her departure.

The next day, Michaela and I were performing in "Laugh at Love," a radio-style comedy revue show for which I'd written some material. The production was upstairs at Caliente Pizza in Castle Shannon. Jenny and Mary both had tickets. Afterward, Jenny texted to say that though Mary was "nice to her" in the crowd, she was clearly in a mood, barely laughed, and kept making snide comments during my segment. It was my first run at standup. The fact that Mary not only had been critical of my performance, but had been publicly so, felt like a yellow jacket sting straight to the heart. The more I thought about it, the madder I got. I was so pissed off that my ears were wiggling.

I had reached my breaking point. I called Mary and got straight to the point: "Mare what in the actual fuck is going on?"

Mare said, and I will never forget the words, "Meg we are not okay. You know that right?"

"Of course we aren't good," I said. "I have no idea why, but you are being a complete bitch to me."

Mary's voice assumed its raised, airing of grievances tone: "Meg, I have been so sick. On top of that, I could be getting laid off. I reached out to you, and my so-called best friend never bothered to call."

Now this made me livid. As a redhead, when I get properly pissed, my face and ears get hot, my face gets red, everything feels warm. I knew I had called Mary a million times—not to mention the texts and Facebook messages. I took a deep breath—an admittedly half-assed effort to calm myself—then let out a series of annoyed, sarcastic, stage laughs: "Hah, hah, hah."

Mare let me have the floor; she knew me well enough, even after a week of semi-estrangement, that a crying fit was on the way. But this time there would be no tears, just venom: "Oh, I didn't call? Come on, does that even sound like me? You need to read your damn texts and listen to your damn voicemail. Try checking Facebook Messenger for once! How hard is it to click on the damn app on your phone? I don't even know how many damn messages I've left." Then a beat. "The benefit of the doubt would be nice after twenty plus years."

Silence on the other end of the line.

"Well," Mary said. "If you say you called, Meg, maybe you did, but I sure as hell didn't hear from you."

"'Maybe' my ass!" I said. "I called you a shit ton. And if I didn't, and it's out of character, why wouldn't you have driven over to see what was up instead of being petty, bordering on the ignore train? You need to go to your phone provider and get your phone checked."

"I don't know what to say, Meg," Mary said.

A first for her.

It had been a hell of a Friday and Saturday. The next morning, I tried to sleep in (always a challenge with Max in bed next to me). When I first heard the phone ringing, the sound blended into the dream I was having. It kept ringing and ringing. I got the message and answered. Mary was in tears, in full-on apologetic monologue mode:

"Meg, I woke up and went straight to Verizon. My phone was jacked; they had to fix it. I finally got all my texts and voicemails. I listened to all, like, seven hundred of your frantic messages. I'm so sorry. It didn't seem like you to not call or text. I didn't know what the hell was up with you."

"Mare," I said. "It's okay. I'm just so relieved that you know I wasn't blowing you off. You're my best friend. You know I could never blow you off!"

"With the bronchitis and the job stuff, it all, just, like, clicked. Like, 'Oh, now Meg is blowing me off, too!'"

"You know I would never do that, Mare. You know that I love you and care about you and I would never not call and write and check in. You are such a big part of my life."

"I love you, too," Mary said. "Please let me take you to Carmella's for brunch and mimosas. We need to catch up. I miss you! I messed up! Let me know when I can swing by and get you!"

Mary wasn't talking about next week or the week after, but that very morning. It never occurred to me to decline, or to dwell on Mary's anger. Yes, the coldness and all the little digs hurt, but they weren't aimed at me. Instead, based on what she was going through and her damn phone randomly going into a vegetative state, Mary had constructed a Meg "straw man"—and she had all but burned that version of me in effigy.

We needed a damn hang. Our brunch at Carmella's Plates and Pints, owned by our friend Carmella Salem, wound up lasting most of the day. We hugged it out, caught up, drank several strawberry jalapeño margaritas, and vowed to always give each other the benefit of the doubt.

Mary and I had known each other for so long, and were so close, we were like different versions of the same character in a play. It was easy to take for granted how fragile, how vulnerable to misunderstandings and technical snafus, our bond—or any bond—could be.

Even besties need to work constantly to communicate, to get on the same page, to make sure that things don't go off the rails. Even then, bumps and snags are going to come up. Mary and I had both been too stubborn, too proud, to reach through the fog of hurt and make sure we were understood.

The whole time Mary and I were "estranged," I was miserable and cried and snapped at people. I should have told myself, "You need her; find a way to work it out." The foolishness was on both of us.

Of course, as we should have known—this was right before COVID changed everything in so many ways—it isn't just communication that is fragile, but life. We do well to live generously. Lead with compassion. Work out the details later.

7. CHEESECAKE AND DEVASTATION

It was August 2021. We had retreated from the real world into the Cheesecake Factory on the South Side, where we had promptly ordered cocktails. It was great to be in a restaurant again, even if the COVID-19 infection numbers were, once again, rising.

In March 2020, COVID had seemingly fallen out of the sky like a plague of snakes and stuck its fangs into life as we knew it. The doors and windows of the world closed and locked overnight. The school-aged kids got the worst of it. For many kids, remote education was no education at all. Max, who needed learning support, struggled mightily. There were exceptions—Michaela, tech savvy, ever-organized, was happy as a clam learning from her room. Kennedy and Daunte fell somewhere between those two poles, but it was a struggle. This was not the fault of the teachers, many of whom worked tirelessly to ford the rushing waters of separation. When it came to distance learning, more often than not, distance won the day.

The employment world, too, was a field of shit. Mary had been laid off just before lockdown. Out of desperation, she sucked up her pride and sought temp and temp-to-perm positions in real estate. Though she was fortunate to find any work at all, she entered into a state of chronic underemployment. Though I didn't lose my job, I was furloughed for two months.

Theater, which had been an outlet for both of us, came to a screeching halt. By then, Michaela had caught the acting bug, and her production of "The Addams Family" was canceled right before opening night. Two of my shows, "Around the World in Eighty Days" and "A Wrinkle in Time," were also scratched.

With Mary, I was worried we would lose our connection because, at first, nobody was leaving their homes at all. Instead, the experience just made us closer. The two of us spoke and texted every day. Then, as many people did, we started to do FaceTime and Zoom hangs where we would drink wine and talk. This felt novel at first, as did wearing masks in public and group settings. The first few months of the pandemic engendered a kind of camaraderie: we were all in uncharted territory, stuck in our homes, and we needed our friends and family more than ever.

Later, when restaurants opened up with restrictions, Mary and I would meet at Carmella's, perch on the bumpers of our cars, and eat brunch with carryout mimosas. We even bought Carmella T-shirts to help support our friend's restaurant. It sounds crazy, but it was fun. True friends will always find a way, and so it was with Mary and me.

Of course, we were all locked down because COVID was deadly. Tens of thousands of people were succumbing to virus-related causes every month in the US alone. Even if you didn't watch or read the news, it was common to hear through family and friends and on social media about people getting really sick, going on ventilators, and dying. My parents' longtime next-door neighbor, an unfailingly kind man, contracted the virus at a family Thanksgiving celebration in 2020 and died a few weeks later. This is how it was.

Back at the Cheesecake Factory, the server brought us our food: a chicken Caesar salad for Mary and a Mexican wrap for me.

"August" by Taylor Swift was playing at a notch above medium volume, and the hook caught me: "I can see us lost in the memory / August slipped away into a moment in time / 'Cause it was never mine." This felt appropriate, as Mary was talking about Ryan, whom she had married almost exactly twenty years before.

"Aren't they supposed to play happy songs at restaurants?" Mary said, as she forked around her salad. "Who wants to listen to this depressing nonsense?"

"But her voice is nice," I said. "It's got kind of a dreamy thing going on."

Mary jabbed her fork into space: "There it is! 'You were never mine.' But he *was* mine, and then he checked out, so I'm moving on. I can't wait until I can actually move."

I took a bite of my wrap. "How is that going?"

"The new job is great," Mary said. She had recently accepted a new position at a real estate management firm in Homestead. The pay was decent and there was a good chance for advancement. "I'm already pricing furniture. The first thing I'm going to get is a damn bed.

I've been sleeping in a chair for so long that it seems normal. How does that sound?"

"Well," I said through my food, "I'm so happy for you about the job. The chair part sounds pretty sad, though."

"Right?" Mary said. "But, Meg, you know I'm not sad. I'm pissed. And I'm not going to give up. I'm going to keep working my ass off until I get the life I want."

"Amen," I said, and took another bite of my wrap.

"Amen, hell yeah," Mary said. "I mean, look at Steve. He's your husband, but he has moved into his own damn unit in the house. You live at 721 Lincoln Run Road. Steve lives at 721 Lincoln Run, Apartment 2B."

I was laughing; it felt so good to laugh.

"I'm going to get him a sign," Mary said. "With a big damn arrow pointing down to the basement where the man lives."

I almost spat out my food.

"But *we're* doing better," I said when I could talk again.

"Who's doing better? You and Steve?" Mary said. The cackle. "Men are such fools."

"You and me," I said.

"Things are *looking* good for me," Mary said, "but I can't get complacent because I'm still new. I need to stay on my grind because I *need* to move. This job is my path out. For you, it's about maintaining; that's different."

I had been back at my job at All-State Career School for more than year. Because commercial driver's license drivers were deemed essential, we were back on site relatively early. We took precautions in the form of masks and daily forehead temperature checks.

The tradeoff, in terms of money and quality of life, was worth it. I'm a people person, and my colleagues and clients at All-State made my work life worth living. No, it wasn't the career I had imagined for myself back at Point Park, but helping people get their lives on track was the kind of work I could get my heart behind.

When we were finished with our entrées, we ordered another round of drinks, a Corona Light with lime for me and a green tea shot for Mary, and, after some real deliberation—it was between the Cinnabon Cinnamon Swirl, for old time's sake, and the White Chocolate Raspberry Truffle—Mary ordered a slice of cheesecake. Mary was diabetic, but she had a sweet tooth, and this would be her real indulgence for the evening.

When the drinks and cheesecake slide arrived, Mary steered us into harder conversational territory: "I think it's total shit that companies are requiring proof of vaccination for people to keep their jobs."

This new subject was either brave or reckless, and maybe it was both. Mary knew, well, that COVID vaccines were a rare, serious point of disagreement for us.

After the vaccine was introduced in December 2020, there was hope. Vaccination meant that most people who were older, or who had preexisting conditions, no longer had to fear for their lives. Likewise, the rest of us could sleep a little better knowing that, if we contracted COVID, we would almost certainly live to act in another play, or go back to work, or whatever our "thing" was.

When, in the spring of 2021, I had an opportunity to get vaccinated, it was a no-brainer. I had older parents and in-laws, not to mention two children and my niece Mia, who had been living in Europe since 2016, but with whom I spoke as often as possible. Moreover, I had a public-facing job. Every day, I interacted with people from every conceivable background and family situation. I needed to protect myself, my family, my colleagues, and my clients.

On the surface, Mary's circumstances were similar: She had Kennedy and Daunte to care for and had a job that required her to be in an office part-time. Mary, who was diabetic and had lost her sister to diabetes-related causes, was at least as cautious as I was: She wore at least one mask, sometimes two. Early on, when we were told the virus was spread through touch, she wore plastic gloves and sanitized her hands seemingly every five seconds. Still, Mary was hesitant to get the vaccine.

Mary's concerns were threefold. Number one was what she called the "fear of the unknowns with the vaccine." It was true that the vaccine had been rush-developed. At the time, there were rumors circulating about the vaccine's origins, the lack of testing, and possible health risks, including heart attack. Mary's line was, "I need more information or it's a 'hell no.'"

Mary's second concern was the vaccine's side effects. Regardless of whether you got the Pfizer or the Moderna version, you needed to get two shots staggered by a few weeks. After the first injection, many people came down with a headache, body aches, and a fever. It was common to feel like shit for up to a day as your body reacted to the small amount of COVID included in the shot. Yes, that was part of how the vaccine worked—it woke your immune system to the threat of the new virus—but this scared many people off. Once, when Mary had gotten a flu shot, she became extremely ill. She was understandably wary about how her body would react to the presence of this new, powerful vaccine in her blood.

Last was the racial piece. Mary was Black. Whatever your views on the state of race relations in the US, the history of race-based inequality in healthcare is undeniable. There was no question that most doctors, regardless of race, meant well and wanted the best for their patients. To what extent, though, were they sensitive to the needs and concerns of the Black community, or of Black women? This was a valid question. Mary was distrustful of the public health system in the US. Combined with her other reservations, this was enough to make her vaccine-hesitant.

Mary's job wasn't requiring proof of vaccination, though, but the fact that any company would do so was just a bridge too far for her.

"No employer has the right to tell me what to do with my body, Meg," Mary said, between bites of cheesecake.

"I can understand that," I said. "But what if you get someone sick? What if the whole business has to shut down because everyone has COVID?"

Mary again held her fork aloft, saber-like. "What if *I* get someone sick? How about, 'What if *someone* gets *me* sick?' And I'm not just talking about in the office, Meg. This is property management; I'm dealing with the damn public."

I thought I had Mary here. "Isn't that a reason to get the vaccine?" I said.

"No," Mary said. "It isn't. It shows that everyone is at risk. And you can get and spread the virus even if you've had a vaccine, so it's not like that solves anything." She took a bite of cheesecake.

I thought it best, in the moment, to hold my tongue: We were at a restaurant and I needed to keep things simpatico. The truth was, though, that I was terrified for Mary. Until recently, she had been working part-time from her computer.

Now that things had opened up, she would be expected to do property visits. On top of that, her children would be back at school full time. All of this would increase Mary's exposure to the virus. That was scary in and of itself, but Mary was also diabetic, which made her high risk. Mary, who had been one of her sister Karen's primary caretakers, knew better than most people that diabetes didn't play.

We finished our drinks, paid, and began our walk to the car. As we walked, the vague feeling of dread that had come over me in the restaurant hardened into something like panic. Mary was my best friend, and she was risking her life—needlessly. I began listing the reasons she should get the vaccine.

"Forget about work," I said. "Think about your role as a mother. You need to be there for Kennedy and Daunte. Think about your hopes and dreams. You want to get out of the damn house you share with Ryan. How are you going to be able to do that if you get sick? Think about me, Mare. You are my person and my life wouldn't be the same without you."

"Time-out," Mary said, her tone cold. "Who said anything about me dying?"

"I just said I was worried," I said.

"No," Mary said. "You started listing people who would be screwed if I caught COVID and died. That's fucked up, Meg."

"But you're high risk," I pleaded.

"It's not like I'm going around letting people breathe on me," Mary said. "And that vaccine is a risk, too! I don't know why you can't see that."

"I haven't seen anything about people dying of the vaccine," I said. "I know more than one person who has died of COVID."

"I'll Facebook Message you some articles," Mary said.

"Fine," I said. "Send me the damn articles! But will you at least consider getting the vaccine? It's summer now, but the numbers are going to get worse in the fall—they always do."

"I'll think about it, Meg," Mary said. "But please let it drop. I don't want to talk about this the whole way back to your place."

"Please do think about it," I said.

"Didn't I just say, 'I'll think about it'? What the hell else do you want?"

"I want you to tell me you're going to get the vaccine!"

"We don't even know what's in the shot!"

For the good of the ride home, and our friendship, I kept my mouth shut. The mood had been soured, though, and the drive to my place was silent. We both needed some space to process.

As I made my way from Mary's Kia to the part of the house I occupied, I felt helpless—like my time with Mary was slipping away and there was nothing I could do to stop it. How could I be so damn powerless to avert a fate I felt in my gut was coming? This feeling is as real now as I write this as it was almost three years ago.

Intellectually, I know the failure was neither mine nor Mary's. Still, in light of what happened, I have never been able to stop, completely, from re-litigating the argument. Maybe if I had said something different, maybe if I had used a different approach . . . . Maybe I should have just opted out of the conversation so the night could have ended on a more harmonious note.

Often, we delude ourselves into thinking that we have the power to alter the course of another person's fate. Sometimes, we do. More often than not, though, our reach exceeds our grasp. We cannot get our hands around whatever it is that makes a person who they are, or act in the way they do. That doesn't mean we should stop grasping. To grasp, to try, is to love.

8. TWIN DREAMS

The last two times I saw Mary feel almost like dreams now, at once vivid and, maddeningly, just beyond reach.

In September 2021, I was cast as the cockney maid, Ida, in "See How They Run," a silly farce with lots of door slams and mayhem. It was an outdoor performance at the South Park Little Theater.

Mary and I each went out of our way to watch each other perform. It meant so much to know that someone would laugh, hard, at the funny bits, would whoop it up for my bow, would appreciate the hard work, team playing, and, yes, talent that went into making each and every performance a success.

On this particular night, Mary and our friend Nikki McGann were supposed to come together. I knew better than to expect Mary to be out there before curtain. Anyway, I was busy scuttling around backstage in my little maid costume, making sure my tea tray was set, hoping for a clear night. After my first entrance, though, I still didn't see Mary and Nikki. People in the audience might think that actors don't sneak glances out at the crowd, but we do. Though I knew it was possible that I just hadn't located my friends, and though I had faith in them—Mary may have been pathologically late, but she usually came through—I felt uneasy.

It was only later, from the darkness, that I saw Nikki with her lawn chair; from this, I was able to deduce that Mary was either in the audience or would soon be. It was like a calm instantly came over me.

Though I never did see Mary that night—she had to sneak out before curtain call to pick up Kennedy—more than once, I heard her trademark cackle loud and clear. Later, she sent me the sweetest messages that made my whole night. My bestie had come through for me.

It was the last time Mary would see me perform.

The next month, with fall foliage daubing Pittsburgh's hills bright yellow, orange, and red,

Mary and I were invited to a Halloween party at our friends Nicole Zalak and Ian Scully-Szejko's home. In theory, vaccination or a negative COVID test was required for all guests, but no one stood at the door and checked. The theme was "dress as a person from history—with a twist." (No, a KN95 mask didn't count as a twist.)

For Mary, celebrations and holidays were memories for Mary, moments to capture, reasons for a new outfit, so she went "big." Mary wanted badly to experience life to the max; it was almost as though, as with my sister Katie, she knew she had limited time and needed to make each moment count.

In our usual way, Mary and I deliberated over the costume options for the better part of a month. We were actors, and actors, almost by definition, love a good theme. We finally settled on Cleopatra for Mary and Marie Antoinette for me. A family favorite growing up was the 1982 British TV adaptation of "The Scarlet Pimpernel" starring Ian McKellen and Jane Seymour. (This was an improvement over the Jane Goodall "National Geographic" specials that had been television events for us before we got a VCR.)

Brainstorming costume ideas and finding clothes that actually worked were two different things. My body shape had changed drastically from its college-era form (no body fat and tiny boobs) to, well, curvy and top-heavy. Often, clothing didn't fit and things wouldn't zipper because of my bust. I ordered and returned at least three Marie Antoinette costumes. It got to the point that I contemplated blue body paint in lieu of a corset.

"That's a hell no," Mary had said. "This isn't *Hair*."

"I'm getting desperate, Mare!" I said.

At the absolute last minute, a suitable top arrived in the mail.

For her part, Mary was also struggling to find something that fit, looked cute, and didn't break the bank. This would require a shopping mission—for which we were, of course, both game. True to form, the pop-up Halloween store we settled on was crowded, picked over, and overpriced. There was a little boy outside the entrance yelling and trying to kick his mom in the shins.

"It's Damien from *The Omen*," I deadpanned.

Mary was more direct: "If that mama doesn't whoop his ass, I may get out and do it for her!"

We each did several laps before finding pieces that remotely worked. Finally, we found a sexy Cleo for Mary (the last one), and a sexy, short ballerina tutu to "sexy up" and modernize the beheaded French queen for me. Our costumes were complete.

At last, the night of the Halloween party arrived. Given Mary's predilection for tardiness, I originally said I would see her there. Nicole and Ian's house was within my comfort zone and I wanted to be at least close to on-time. Mary, though, insisted that she pick me up: "Meg, there will be no parking! I will be on time. I'll pick you up. I'd rather go together."

"Great," I said. "Call or text when you're on your way."

This "surrender" was something of a calculated move on my part. I wanted Mary to go to the party. As her work life had grown busier and her personal life more complicated, the truth is that I wasn't seeing as much of Mary. I knew that us going separately to the party might give her an out, and I needed to see my friend.

I'd gone back and forth with my hair. My wig was more Dolly Parton in "The Best Little

Whorehouse in Texas" than pre-revolution Paris. I finally asked my friend Mandy Westerbeck to do my hair; she is incredible and made it work. I took forever doing my makeup, lacing the corset, and adding beauty marks to my face and fake blood to my neck. I now knew the reason why women in old paintings looked so damn uncomfortable: They were so tied down, literally, that they couldn't breathe. It made no difference whether I sat or stood. Finally I just balanced myself on the edge of a chair, took short breaths, and settled into waiting for Mary.

The party started early: 6:30 p.m. I didn't expect or need to be the first person there. I also knew that when Mary said she would be on time, what she really meant was that she would actively work to be less late. At least, that's what I hoped. 6:00 rolled round, then 6:30, then 7:00, then 7:30. So much for "less late." My multiple texts yielded no response. Finally, I broke down and called.

"Mare Mare," I said, working hard to keep my tone light. "It's almost eight. Are you on your way? What is your ETA?"

There was a long, pregnant pause. "Meg," Mary said. "Don't be mad. I was keeping up with the Kardashians. I'm getting ready to jump into the shower right now!"

"Oh God, Mare," I said, perched as I was like a Madame Alexander doll with unbendable limbs.

"I'm sorry!" Mary said.

I knew what some of our friends at the party would be thinking: Mary strikes again. I was annoyed, too, but I knew it wasn't personal. Part of being in any long-term relationship, be it family, marriage, or a decades-long friendship, is modulating your expectations and emotional reflexes. I'm not saying we should tolerate physical or emotional abuse; what I mean is that some aspects of our behavior come down to who we are as people. None of us is perfect, and, in the end, it is the patchwork of strengths and weaknesses that make us the distinctive and memorable characters we are. I let bygones be bygones and called an Uber.

I arrived. Everyone loved my costume, but people kept asking where my "partner in crime" was. Mary and I were a set: frick and frack; wherever one was, the other was usually close by. I also felt Mary's absence as my foil. In social situations, I have a hard time making the first move; I need time to warm up (and for the alcohol to take effect). In this case, the problem was worsened by the fact that I could barely breathe without ripping my corset, which I could feel beginning to splinter, thread by thread. My friend Steve had made amazing Jello shots, so those were helping. Still, I kept crab walking to the window—forward motion wasn't working too well—to check for sexy, Black Cleopatra.

Finally, my phone buzzed. I picked up: "Meg, I'm on the street. Do you care if I come? I have another commitment after this!"

Under normal circumstances, I wouldn't have pushed Mary—if she wasn't feeling it, no big deal. But we hadn't seen each other since summer, a very long time for us, and there was just something inside me saying that I couldn't back down on this one. Also, we were both in fucking costume. What's the point of brainstorming costume ideas, getting dressed up as damn Marie Antoinette and Cleopatra, only to take a pass and move on to another "commitment"?

I wanted to say something like "Uh, yes I do care if you don't come!" but I knew from years of experience that venting would be counterproductive. So I tried the "kill her with kindness" approach: "Mare Mare," I said, almost teasingly. "Come in for one drink. I miss you. Everyone is asking about you. Are you in your costume?"

When Mary finally arrived in her Cleopatra finery, it was like the belle of the ball walking in: The whole party stopped as Mary made her grand, stunning entrance. As I had been watching these slow walks for years, I can say with confidence that this was a particularly impressive performance, not the least because Mary was clearly having a hard time moving in her costume.

For my part, reunited with my partner, I felt free of the self-imposed shackles of shyness. Mary and I, Cleopatra and Marie Antoinette, deposited ourselves at the snacks and liquor table—in part to minimize the need to move—and held court, telling crazy stories from our past. Everyone was laughing and telling their own stories, too. Our friend Greg Pegher was dressed as Harry Houdini with his hands tied. We challenged him to find ways to take shots without using his hands; it was hilarious. We took a million selfies as usual. In the end, Mary stayed for far longer than one drink.

The next few weeks were busy for both of us. No problem, I figured, we'd get together around Thanksgiving. Mary tested positive for COVID just before the holiday. Five days later she started having trouble breathing and went to the emergency room. She would never recover.

If I had known the party was my last time to truly spend with Mary, I would have hugged her again, taken a million more pictures, and never let her strut out the door. Something I have learned to do over time is reframe the way I see situations: Instead of focusing on the negative, I try to find the positive. The fact is that Mary almost didn't show up at all. I will be forever grateful that she did.

9. SUNDOWN

As autumn strengthens its hold on Western Pennsylvania, moisture from Lake Erie rises and is shaped into flat, stratus clouds, which are blown south. Behind the Alleghenies, the clouds linger and thicken into a watercolor mosaic of softer and darker shades of gray. As the days grow shorter and the nights longer, the combination of diffuse light and actual darkness can result in whole weeks without direct sun. On the ground, around Thanksgiving, my world also became bleak.

On Sunday, November 14, an overcast day, Mary posted a quote from life coaching and inspiration site Women Working: “Every Woman needs a ‘No Matter What’ friend. Someone they can call No Matter What. Someone they can vent to No Matter What. Someone she doesn’t have to explain herself to,

No Matter What." She tagged the photo with five hearts and six "100" emoji.

On November 15, another cloudy day, Mary tested positive for COVID. At first, Mary didn't seem overly concerned because she knew other people whose experience with COVID had been more like a bad cold. Nevertheless, anytime you got COVID, you knew you were dealing with a wild card. By November 2021, almost everyone knew someone who had died from the virus or complications relating to it. Likewise, most people knew at least one person whose bout, or bouts, with the virus had developed into the mysterious, chronic long COVID.

A hint of Mary's growing concern is evident in her last Facebook post on Tuesday, November 16. Another quote from Women Working: "Sisters Forever: As Sisters, We take care of each other, We watch out for each other, & Comfort each other through the good times and the bad times. Sister, I Love You." She dedicated her post to her sister Iris Johnson Armstrong and "sister in heaven" Karen Johnson.

On November 18, which was cloudy with drizzle, I wrote, "Hey, Mare, I tried calling you today and Tuesday. How are you feeling?"

On Saturday, November 20, which was mostly cloudy, Mary went to the emergency room at Jefferson Hospital, in Jefferson Hills, for labored breathing. She was treated, I'm not sure exactly how or with what, and released.

Sunday evening, I again wrote to Mary: "Hey Mare, just tried to call? How are you feeling? My brother is in town. Had to wear a mask around everyone. A student I met with on Monday for an hour called to tell my boss that he tested positive. I can still work because I'm fully vaccinated, no fever or symptoms, but had to get a test today."

On Monday, a partly cloudy day, Mary was admitted to the hospital. There was concern that Mary would stop breathing in her sleep because her oxygen and blood sugar levels were both really bad. Visits to COVID-positive patients weren't permitted; I begged to be able to put on a hazmat suit and go in, but the answer was a flat "no" until Mary tested negative.

On Tuesday, which was mostly cloudy, I wrote to Mary: "My Mare Mare . . . I'm so sorry I'm not by your bedside right now. I wish Ryan would have sent me a text. I felt like something was wrong when I could not reach you. Praying for a speedy recovery. Love you my other half, XO."

This time, Mary responded: "Love you, too, they are keeping me in the hospital."

Mary's oxygen levels were still not good. She was being treated with corticosteroid therapy, for which the tradeoff was soaring blood sugar.

The exact link between COVID-19 and diabetes is still not well understood. What is known is that people with diabetes who are infected with COVID are far more likely to be hospitalized, to be intubated, and to die from complications set into motion by the virus. Instead of fighting just the virus, diabetics, and in particular those whose disease is uncontrolled, find themselves in a two-front war: Their immune systems are already compromised; their cardiovascular systems are operating under greater stress. Worse, COVID and diabetes can play off each other, exacerbating symptoms, triggering "cascading" effects, and worsening outcomes by an order of magnitude.

Mary knew she was diabetic, and she had seen firsthand through her sister Karen the devastation the disease could wreak upon even middle-aged people. My sense is that Mary didn't take her diabetes as seriously as she might have because she was still just in her mid forties, paid attention to her figure, and didn't feel sick. Mary had no way of knowing that this snake, COVID-19, would drop out of the sky. When it did, she had only a vague awareness of her increased level of risk as a diabetic. It was all so abstract, and she was in the prime of her life.

On Wednesday, which was cloudy with rain, I wrote, "Good morning, Mare. How are you feeling? Any improvement?" When Mary didn't respond, my concern deepening, I followed up, "Hey, Mare. Called your cell and your room phone. Is everything okay? What is Kennedy's number?"

Thanksgiving evening: "Trying to reach you. Are you okay? I'm worried; such a hard Thanksgiving. I called your cell and your room phone yesterday and today."

As I would later learn from her brother, Craig, Mary had been moved to the intensive care unit. She was kept there for a few days, and, when her oxygen and blood sugar numbers stabilized, returned to the step-down COVID-19 unit.

Thereafter, Mary continued to have only sporadic access, and ability to use, her phone. Craig secured her a hospital iPad in the hope that FaceTimes with friends and family would boost her spirits. Mary, though, refused to use it—the "visual" component would have just been too hard, on a number of levels.

For the next week and a half, Mary was fighting. I established a connection with Mary's nurses and was able to call and check on her condition. She had good days and bad days. Breathing was a constant struggle and concern. Depending on her oxygen levels, she was on either CPAP and BIPAP, with short experiments with breathing on her own. The nurses also pushed Mary to breathe without assistance—they kept emphasizing that if she didn't improve, she would have to be intubated.

The dilemma Mary faced was rooted in the fact that she could never catch her breath. It was a catch-22: Mary couldn't breathe comfortably without assistance, but any mask or breathing tube caused her to panic. The solution was to add an anti-anxiety medication to Mary's drip. The tradeoff was that, when I did get to speak with her, Mary seemed loopy and disconnected, a situation that was exacerbated by the unsettling echo of the "diver mask" with which she had been fitted.

Somewhere in this period, Mary and I spoke for the last time. She was recognizably Mary, but the fighting spirit, the brightness that had been as much of a part of her personality as her ever-shifting hairstyles and Tina Turner strut, had dimmed. The world had kept pushing against her, and she had kept pushing back with the tenacity of a woman who knew she deserved more than she got, but now she was sick, exhausted, and despondent.

"I'm dying," she said through the diver mask.

I could feel the chill from the palms of my hands to the soles of my feet.

"You're not dying," I said.

I needed to find a way to shift Mary's perspective, to help her see herself as a party, an agent, in what was happening—not as a person to whom all of this terror was being unleashed.

"You're fighting. You were in the ICU, but you've been in step-down for more than a week now. You're making baby steps."

"No, Meg," Mary struggled to say. "Listen to me: I'm dying."

Again, I felt the chill.

"Mare," I pleaded. "They have you on so many drugs. You aren't yourself. You can't be yourself right now because your body is fighting this virus."

"You're not listening! You're not listening, Meg!"

"I am listening, Mare!" I said. But I couldn't give in, couldn't stop grasping: "I don't want you to die. You don't want to die. So you have to keep fighting like you have been. You are so strong. You have so much to live for. Kennedy, Daunte, Iris, Craig. You love your family so much. You have been through so much, and you have always kept pushing."

"You have to listen to me, Meg!"

"I love you, Mare! You are my best friend and I love you!"

"I love you, too, Meg. You know that. I'm just tired. I'm so tired."

At the time, I couldn't admit to myself that Mary knew. I can now accept that she did. This conversation will haunt me for the rest of my life.

On December 7, another overcast day, Mary's nurses reported that she had her best day yet. She walked a bit, ate better than she had been eating. I was feeling heartened and optimistic.

The next day, Craig called: Overnight, Mary had gone into cardiac arrest and "coded," not once, but twice. The doctors had brought her back, moved her to the ICU, and put her into a medically induced coma to give her body an opportunity to rest and recover.

She was no longer COVID-positive.

10. THE DIMMING HOUR

From there we passed into a kind of Dimming Hour, the period just before dusk when the unseen sun begins to set behind the overcast sky-scape, the diffuse light growing more diffuse still, the hues of gray darkening into a kind of blue.

Initially, the nurses were encouraging. They said they had seen COVID patients, as sick or sicker than Mary, recover. She just needed more time.

The very minute Mary's nurses said we could visit, Craig called me. I left work as soon as my boss would let me and raced to be with my best friend. I was certain that when she heard my voice and looked at me, she would be back.

When I was in front of the hospital, flowers in hand, Craig called again. His tone was measured: "Meg, I just left from seeing Mare. They were testing her body for responses. She was only responding on one side. Either she is too sedated, still, or she has had a stroke, to what level we don't know."

Until that point, I had been thinking that Mary would be weak or fragile but still Mary. I thought I would be coming in to talk with her as she slowly woke up. I would hold her hand and tell her I was there and that everything would be okay.

I knew from my experience with my sister Katie what to expect in the ICU, but there is no way to prepare for seeing a person you love in an oxygen mask, with tubes everywhere. Mary looked so small. Usually she would be the one to comfort me—"C'mon, Meg"—but there she was, so peaceful, unable to speak. You find yourself fantasizing in such moments: Maybe *this* will get through to her; maybe then all this can be reversed, taken back, rewound, and we can walk out together and life will be as it was before.

In this period, I sat with Mary after work every day, and all day on the weekend, sometimes alone and sometimes with visitors. I enjoyed both, but secretly enjoyed my time with just Mary. I would stay until close, tidy up her room, fix her blankets, straighten her hair, put on music that wasn't "easy listening," talk and gossip with her, and reassure her. I let Mary know I nearly peed my pants trying to come from work and locate a women's room in the maze-like hospital in a one-piece pants suit. She would look at me, squeeze my hand, and her vital signs would change. I believe she knew I was there.

* * *

One day the doctors ushered Craig, Mary's nephew Christian, and me into a room. We got Iris and Ryan on the phone. You never want to be ushered into a tiny room or corner of the ICU ward because it usually means bad news. Although I had experience with this, I had adjusted to our new normal and was totally unprepared.

The doctor explained that they had run tests. Mary had suffered a severe stroke in the "thinking" part of her brain. One possibility would be to transport her via helicopter to Allegheny General Hospital on Pittsburgh's North Side for brain surgery—an attempt to restore oxygen to the affected parts of Mary's brain. Even if the surgery were successful, the prognosis would be mixed. The brain was so complex. Mary would live, but no one could be certain of her quality of life.

The doctor left the room. The initial sentiment was to go for it. Mary had been a fighter all her life, and it only seemed right that we should give her a chance to live.

As we were quietly deliberating, Mary's main ICU nurse, who had been standing on the periphery, came over to us. She was a small woman, dressed in dark blue scrubs and crocs. A mask obscured her face and drew focus to her gray eyes, flecked with cobalt blue. Time and its workings had exerted a pull on the visible parts of the nurse's face: her forehead was creased, the lines only somewhat concealed. The skin around her eyes had slackened. The power of the eyes, themselves, undiminished, pure, hot like the blue part of a flame.

"I have to speak up," the nurse said in a voice just barely hushed. "I don't think you know all the information. I'm going to be a little bit blunt with you, but this comes from a place of care."

We homed in on the nurse's eyes and steeled ourselves for whatever would come next.

"If Mary survives the procedure. *If* she survives," the nurse repeated, and punctuated her point by withholding the standard blink of an eye—"at best, she will live in a nursing home unable to walk, talk, eat on her own. That is how she will be."

The nurse moved her gaze from Craig to me and back again. "You need to understand that there is no chance for better. The brain is just so fragile. Damage from a severe stroke like this can't be reversed; that is just the nature of stroke."

The nurse's eyes shifted. Whereas before the blue shone through, now the moderating, humanizing gray predominated. She spoke more softly now: "I can see how much you love Mary, and I don't want you to put her, or yourselves, through all of that out of some hope that is just not realistic. I just wanted someone to be honest."

Another pause.

"You can give her family time to come in and see her. We can keep her comfortable, and not put her through trauma that won't bring back Mary."

This nurse was incredibly brave, speaking up for Mary when she herself could not. We all went to our separate corners. I was crying so hard; I was hyperventilating and wailing and couldn't stand. My mind went blank. Oh God, no. Oh God, not Mary. Oh God, she has two wonderful children. She has a brother and a sister who love her dearly. She is my best friend. Oh God, Mary does not deserve this. Mary has given so much of herself to so many people. Oh God, I don't understand; I can't understand.

A long moment passed. When the storm began to settle, one truth became clear to me. Mary, who loved to sing and drive and shop and live, who lived life with more zeal than anyone I had ever met, would never want to exist in a quasi-vegetative state. She would not want her kids to see her that way. It wouldn't be fair to anyone, least of all Mary.

When we reconvened, I was relieved to learn that all of Mary's loved ones felt the same way I did. We agreed to let Mary go.

The sun had set.

* * *

Twilight. The blue hour, in which we say goodbye to the day.

Mary was an organ donor, and she would be kept on life support long enough to find a home for each and every one of her organs that could be donated.

It wasn't a bedside vigil, exactly, as much as a near constant stream of visitors. I had to break into Mary's phone to reach out to some people and was able to guess the pass code in two tries. I arranged pictures around the room. Mare's hair and nails needed some love. We asked our friend Janice, who had previously owned a nail salon, to come and give Mary a manicure. She came with Nikki McGann and gave Mary beautiful ice gold and blue nails. I fixed Mary's hair myself.

In some ways, it felt like we were back in our old place on Swinburne Street: There was a flow of familiar faces. I cannot list all the names, there were so many. Sara Strenk drove all day to sit with Mary. Mary Chess Randolph came and spent a few hours with Mary and me. I was struck by how much Mary's close friend from high school, Rayna Ramseur, looked just like her; they had called each other "twin."

We tried to shield Kennedy and Daunte from everything Mary had gone through, but Kennedy came one day and absolutely grilled the nurses about what had happened and why. She spent some time alone with her mom, sharing a moment and words that will remain only between them.

The hours seemed to move so slowly, then too fast. And then it was night.

11. SAFFRON NIGHT

The morning of December 14, 2021 was clear and cold. There was an iciness to the air that I could not shut out no matter how hard I tried. I wanted desperately to be brave, to be strong, but I was feeling heartbroken, terrified, and beyond angry. I was desperate for a miracle.

This was the day, the day I would have to actually let you go, to comfort your children, your brother, your sister, your family, your friends, to begin to learn to live without you.

You so generously pledged to donate every organ in your small body that could be used to save or help another person.

This was the day we would honor your generosity, your courage, your love.

Your room was crowded with people who loved you, cared about you, would be at a loss without you. A few nurses came in.

They asked if I wanted to say a few words. How could I sum up your beautiful, tenaciously-lived life in just a few words? I was looking at my best friend: a young, talented, vibrant, otherwise healthy woman with so much life ahead. None of it made sense: COVID, diabetes, heart attacks, stroke. I told everyone that you were one of a kind, that the world would never be the same, that I would miss you and love you forever.

I had put together a playlist on my phone for your honors walk to the surgery room. As we began to walk down the corridor to the surgery room, Craig on one side and me on the other, something really beautiful happened. With the music playing, all the doctors and nurses and attendants came out and stood silently along our route. As we turned each new corner, more of the people who made the hospital work emerged from their posts and stood and paid their respects and honored your courage and generosity. I was so proud, so far beyond moved, but still so lost and confused; my mind kept returning to "Why, God, why now?" I kept trying to concentrate, to focus on the idea that I couldn't know, couldn't understand, and that what you needed in this moment was my love. It was devastating and it was beautiful—both of those things at the same time.

When we reached the operating room, Craig and I put on hazmat suits so we could go with you. We didn't want you to be alone. We watched as the doctors removed everything keeping you alive in your body. You took one shallow breath, and you were gone. The brightest light I had come to know in my life went out. All of our memories, all of our stories, all of our time together flashed before my mind.

I know you are with God doing important things, probably still giving people some sass. You are with your parents, with your sister Karen and my sister Katie, but I just want you here. I had imagined us growing old together, being again roommates in the nursing home: "Swinburne Sisters: Senior Edition." I cannot imagine the rest of my life without you. I do not want to imagine the rest of my life without you.

Mare, I miss you so, so much. I love you more than words. You were more than a friend, more than a sister. You were, and are, my "person." Your light continues to shine through Kennedy and Daunte, and me, and everyone who was lucky enough to know you. You live on in the memories, in the stories that I hold in my heart, that I will tell so that they, and you, live on—so that this history will never be lost but will gain new life, so that you, too, will live on.

I love you, my dear friend. Rest easy.

Meg

p.s. I had not peed all morning. On my way out of the hospital, after returning to your room to collect your things, after getting a bite to eat in the café with Mary Kay—I only ate then because I hadn't eaten a thing in forty-eight hours—I snuck behind some cars and peed. I know you were looking down, laughing hysterically. I'm on a damn water pill, forty-seven years old, with two kids. Waiting this long to pee was stupid as hell. I know you understand, though. Pee happens.

ABOUT THE AUTHOR

Megan May graduated from Point Park University in 1997 with a Bachelor of Fine Arts degree. She has been acting and writing since childhood. By day, she works as a financial aid adviser. By night, she can be found on stage at community theaters to which she can easily drive. She lives in West Mifflin, Pennsylvania with her husband, Steve, her son, Max, her dog, Finn, and her cat, Lyra; daughter Michaela, deep into college, is an intermittent resident.

Made in the USA
Middletown, DE
27 June 2024